How To Get Into And Graduate From College in Four Years with

good grades, a useful major,

a lot of knowledge, a little debt,

All
great friends, happy parents,

maximum party attendance,

minimal weight gain,

decent habits, fewer hassles,

a career goal, and a super attitude,

all while remaining extremely cool.

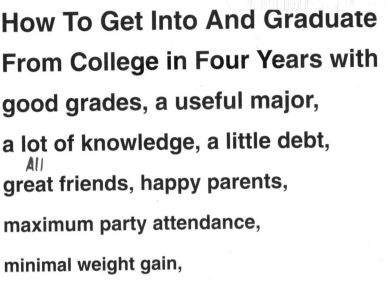

By Martin J. Spethman

Illustrated by Ralph Cabrera

WESTGATE PUBLISHING & ENTERTAINMENT, INC.
Miami, Florida • Omaha, Nebraska

This book is printed on recycled paper.

Cover Design & Book Composition by Westgate Publishing & Entertainment, Inc., Margaret Spethman, Lisa Desmond & Dawna Harris

For information concerning this publication and discount quantity purchases, contact: Westgate Publishing & Entertainment, Inc. Suite 32-109 260 Crandon Blvd Miami, Florida 33149 (305) 361-6862 or 2823 S. 116th Ave. Omaha, Nebraska 68144 (402) 334-6957

ISBN number 0-9633598-0-0.

First edition: 10 9 8 7 6 5 4 3 2 1

Printed in the USA.

CONGRATULATIONS, you have just helped plant a tree. With your purchase of "How to get into and graduate in four years..." Westgate Publishing has arranged with American Forests to plant a tree in one of America's Heritage Forests through the Global ReLeaf Program. Global Releaf is a national education, action, and policy campaign of the American Forests aimed at improving the earth's environment through planting & cultivating more trees and forests. Trees not only cool the earth by helping control carbon dioxide in the atmosphere, they purify air and water, protect watersheds, enhance wildlife habitat, prevent soil erosion and add to the natural beauty of the land.

You can become involved with the Global ReLeaf Organization in a variety of ways:

1. Take part in your communities' tree planting program or if one does not currently exist, alert your community leaders of the need to plant and maintain trees.

2. Become a contributing member of Global ReLeaf. You can learn more about local, national and international policies that effect trees and forests.

3. Make an additional donation to Global ReLeaf and plant more trees by calling 1-900-420-4545. This $5 phone call will plant one tree in a Global ReLeaf forest.

For more information on American Forests/Global ReLeaf Program or to become a member, call (202) 667-3300 or write P.O. Box 2000 Washington, D.C. 20013.

Global ReLeaf is about people taking action now!

PLANT A TREE, COOL THE GLOBE!

WESTGATE PUBLISHING & ENTERTAINMENT, INC.
Miami, Florida • Omaha, Nebraska

This book is dedicated to my family Richard, Virginia, Patricia, Richard Jr., Susan, Kathleen, Joanne and Peggy.

I would like to thank Albert Einstein, Winston Churchill, Martin Luther King, MTV, Hang Gliding, Grizzly Gulch and Key Biscayne each for their inspiration. I would like to thank my old dog Dillion for many a walk in the mountains. A special thanks to Kelly Kreikemeier, Malachy Sullivan and Mike Pallesen for marrying my sisters. A special thanks to Ed Spethman for his editing assistance. I would like to thank my illustrator Ralph Cabrera and his assistants Jude Millien and Steve Montero. I would especially like to thank Ana Banos, Kamran Kadivar, Sharon Morrison and Mike MeLoy for their contributions known and unknown. I would also like to thank American Forests and the Global ReLeaf Organization for their efforts to save the earth by planting trees.

I would like to thank my illustrator Ralph Cabrera and my typography and graphic design experts Margaret Spethman, Lisa Desmond and Dawna Harris. I would like to express my extreme gratitude to the following people who contributed their research and expertise to the book: Colleen Eickelman and Laurie Irvine.

Hi, we're the
Super Perfect Pairs!
We'll see you later
in the book.

Hi, we're the Couch
Potato Couples!
We'll catch you later
in the book.

About the Author:

Martin J. Spethman: Is uniquely qualified to write this book because he made almost every academic mistake known to man while he attended college. The lessons contained herein flow from this five year educational adventure. The author did manage to have a great time in college and graduate from Carroll College in Helena, Montana with a degree in Business Administration. He was born and raised in Omaha, Nebraska and is the founder of Westgate Publishing & Entertainment, Inc. which is a literary works company dedicated to publishing books. Prior to founding Westgate, he lived in Chicago, IL and Miami, FL. and worked in the typesetting field. In 1987, he started and operated a successful typesetting company for three years, MS Language & Technology, Inc. which was sold after reaching sales in excess of a million dollars.

About the Editors:

Colleen Eickelman: Holds a Masters Degree in History and is currently working on her Masters in College Counseling for High School students. She has been a teacher and counselor for 12 years. She is the author and presentor for several College Prep classes and workshops which help prepare students and their parents for college. She has been awarded with the National History Day Recognition Award, the PTSA State Life Award, the 1989 Alice E. Buffet Outstanding Teacher Award and has been listed in Who's Who Among America's Teachers since 1990. She was the recipient of the Bill of Rights Collaborative Teaching Grant in Washington, D.C. and has been the Coach for the National History Day teams from 1984 -1992.

Laurel Irvine: Graduated Cum Laude from the State University of New York with a Bachelor of Arts in History. She received her Masters Degree in Educational Guidance and Counseling from Barry University, Florida in 1975. In 1972, she became a high school Social Studies teacher and a guidance counselor in 1976. In 1985, she assumed the responsibilities of guidance director at Stranahan High School. In 1990, she became a district administrator coordinating the Broward Advisors for Continuing Education (BRACE) program for all district schools, a position she currently holds.

About the illustrator:

Ralph Cabrera: Has a degree in Commercial Art with an emphasis on Advertising. He has taught several courses on Illustration at Miami Dade Community College in Miami, Florida. Currently he is working as a Comic Illustrator for both Marvel and DC comics. His accomplishments are featured in wide varity of Marvel Comic Books including "Silver Surfer", "Captain Planet", and "Quasar".

Photography by Jill Kahn Photo, Miami Beach

TABLE OF CONTENTS

Introduction

INTRODUCTION

"TO REBEL OR TO EXCEL? ....THAT IS THE QUESTION." You can actually do both.

So, you are a little stressed about college, huh? Well, what's your problem? That is not normal. You should be very relaxed about the upcoming college experience, what kind of grades you are going to get, whether or not you will meet good friends, whether you will lose old ones, whether your first choice will accept you, how you're going to pay for college, how you're going to eat while you pay for college, whether or not your parents will be cool while you're in college, your entire future on this planet! Actually, we all know better. You are uptight about leaving your high school and want to go to the principal and request that you be allowed to stay another year. NOT!!!

O.K., how about if you tell me how you feel about leaving high school and going off to college?

☐ It's great

☐ It really #$!%!?

☐ I am not sure

☐ I have not given it much thought

☐ I am nervous

☐ All of the above

Your own feelings please _____

_____

_____

_____

_____

_____

And what are your biggest concerns about going to college?

- ☐ Being too far from home.
- ☐ Being too close to home.
- ☐ Not getting good grades.
- ☐ Not being able to get a job after I graduate.
- ☐ Money.
- ☐ Not being able to play sports.
- ☐ Fitting in.
- ☐ Getting lost.
- ☐ Stress.
- ☐ Money.
- ☐ Not getting accepted into college.
- ☐ Will partying become more important than school?
- ☐ Being able to stand 4 more years of school.
- ☐ Being able to stand 4 more days of school.
- ☐ Being able to stand 4 more words of this book.
- ☐ Money.
- ☐ What am I going to do when I graduate from college?
- ☐ What am I going to do when I don't graduate from college?
- ☐ Making new friends.
- ☐ Losing old friends.
- ☐ Having fun.
- ☐ Not being able to get out of bed for classes.
- ☐ Will there be enough parties?
- ☐ Living on my own.
- ☐ Not having parents take care of everything.
- ☐ Getting a room mate who is a "Surf Nazi".
- ☐ Becoming a "Surf Nazi".
- ☐ Becoming a "Surf Naziette".
- ☐ Not liking my roommate.
- ☐ Too much homework.
- ☐ I have no concerns, I am one with the universe.
- ☐ Choosing the wrong school.
- ☐ Choosing the right wardrobe.
- ☐ Weight gain.
- ☐ Weight loss.
- ☐ Choosing the correct major.
- ☐ Getting dumped by my girlfriend.
- ☐ Getting dumped by my boyfriend.
- ☐ Being an accountable adult.
- ☐ No time for girls.
- ☐ No time for boys.
- ☐ No time for animals.

Please add your own here:

_____

_____

_____

Since you told me what you're thinking about going to college, I am going to tell you what I think. I think you are taking a great first step in going to college. That is, thinking about college early, reading this book, and utilizing your counselor, parental figures and your high school's college prep program to the fullest.

I know some of you might be asking: "What if I do not want to go to college? I am sick of school and I don't want to see another book for as long as I live"!! That is fine. If you think you might want to sit out a year, then by all means do so. It is wise to first discuss this with your parents. Don't freak if they do not agree with you, just listen and discuss it. You are both on the same side.

If you choose not to immediately go on to college, then whatever you do, do not sit around vegging and waste your year off from school. This is the worst thing you could do!!!!! Chances are, you took the break for financial reasons too, so you should be working. If you are lucky and can afford to travel, then go for it. Just do not waste your time and do keep your eye on your long term goals. **If you are not sure "what you want to be when you grow up" college is the greatest place to decide.**

Since this book is about going to college, I am not going to discuss some of the other avenues to higher education. The Armed Forces, Religious Vocations, Technical Schools, etc.. Any one of these can, and will, get you to where you want to go. You must decide where that is and pursue the option that you, with the help of a few others, think will get you there.

Keep in mind, following the guidelines in this book does not guarantee that you will graduate in four years, get good grades, pursue a useful major, have happy parents, gain a lot of knowledge, maintain little debt, make good friends, not miss a party, experience minimal weight gain, acquire a lot of good habits, have fewer hassles, find a career goal and remain extremely cool, but it definitely should get you a lot closer to achieving these goals! Use this book as a platform to issues and information you need to discuss with your counselor, parents or friends. Use this book as a schedule and a notepad to help you organize and prepare for college. Use this book as a guide to handle the college lifestyle once you arrive. Use this book as kindling for a bonfire! Whatever you do, **use this book!!!!**

CHAPTER 1

COLLEGE PREPARATION

You might say to yourself, "Hey, I just made it into high school, why do I have to think about college already?" Well, you don't, so put this book down, tell your guidance counselor to mellow out and leave you alone, and skip school for the rest of the day. And while you're at it, find a shopping cart to live in and make a sign "Will Work For Food" because you might need them later. Actually the reason you want to think about college is very simple. Don't think about college because of your parents. Don't think about college because of your counselors. Don't think about college because of your friends. Think about going to college because of **YOU!!!!!!!!!!**

Making an informed decision about going to college is going to benefit no one more than yourself. Sure, your parents will be happy with a good choice about where you end up for college, if anywhere at all. The knowledge that you will get an education and will eventually be able to support yourself is greatly appreciated by concerned parents. Your counselors will be happy since it is their job to help you in the college selection and application process. However, no one will be happier about you going to college than you!!

Why? Because college is one massive party with all your friends, where you have total freedom to do whatever you want whenever you want, with whomever you want. **In your dreams!** Although parties and freedom are certainly part of any college experience, college really is, two, four even five years of people helping you, help yourself.

Every day, every class, every homework assignment, even every test is going to bring you closer to whatever you want in life. **College is the best chance any high school senior has to assure he or she will be given the opportunity to get exactly what he or she wants out of life.** College is one of the most, if not the most, important educational experience a person can go through, and I don't mean just classes. High school students owe it to themselves to devote the right amount of time to insure they get a fair shot at the university they want to attend. Look at it this way, either you follow the guidelines in this book, supplemented by your counselor's advice and proceed through the college application and research process in a timely and expedient manner, thus guaranteeing an adequate amount of information gathering and responsible action based on this information . . .or . . . you go down to the nearest tattoo shop and have " I really don't want anything out of life and I would like to live at home, not meet anymore friends and work for three dollars an hour for the rest of my life" tattooed to your forehead.

The most important rule for students just embarking on the college selection and application process is to utilize your guidance counselor to the maximum. They have a tremendous amount of information for you. They can walk you through the necessary steps and with the help of books like this one, you can get into college and go on to be the president, or at least go on and have enough money to be able to afford Domino's Pizza whenever you want. Your counselor has set up a program to assist you in the process, make sure you pay attention to the program and use it to the fullest!

If your school does not have a college counseling program or is short on counselors, then you will just have to follow the guidelines in this book and get everything done on your own. Believe me, you can handle it!

In any case, remember, the final responsibility to get all this stuff done is **yours!!!**

So, if you're ready, let's get after it!

My college guidance counselor is_____.

I can find him/her at_____.

Phone #_____

Office Hours:_____-_____ Weekend Hours:_____-_____

My first appointment_____.

Other important contacts I might need to check out: (Public Library, College Admission Offices, relatives or friends that went to college, employers, mentors)

Name: _____	Room #_____
Phone #_____	Office Hours:_____-_____
Name: _____	Room #_____
Phone #_____	Office Hours:_____-_____
Name: _____	Room #_____
Phone #_____	Office Hours:_____-_____
Name: _____	Room #_____
Phone #_____	Office Hours:_____-_____
Name: _____	Room #_____
Phone #_____	Office Hours:_____-_____
Name: _____	Room #_____
Phone #_____	Office Hours:_____-_____

Besides knowing who and where your guidance counselor is and having a copy of this book, there are only five things you must understand and complete in order to get into college. Those are fewer steps to go through than trying to find someone to buy beer for you on a Friday night or finding a date for the Prom.

1. **Developing an extremely cool transcript and resume.**
2. **Deciding where you are going to go to college.**
3. **Analyzing how you are going to pay for college.**
4. **Tests you have to take to get in.**
5. **How to apply.**

So, to help you get organized, we have included this College Preparation Calendar/Check List. As you finish an item, make sure you check it off. Look at the whole calendar and try to jot down tentative dates for the activities.

SOPHOMORE AND/OR JUNIOR YEAR
FALL

Date
Scheduled

Date
Completed

1. Have meeting with your counselor and chart 2 or 3 year plan for courses. Ideally, you have planned a 4 year course when you entered High School. Have a check up and make sure you are on track.

2. Meet with guidance counselor to discuss and/or begin college prep program. Familiarize yourself with all resources for college information (Admissions Tests, Applications, Scholarships, Financial Aid, Workshops, College Catalogs, Computer Software . . .). Make sure you get a booklet about government financial aid programs.

3. Devote some thought to your career interest and follow up with some research. Work on getting involved in extracurricular activities and part time jobs that interest you. Save any money you can.

4. Introduce yourself to the PLAN test by taking a sample one and reviewing the PSAT Computer program if available.

5. Participate, with your parents, in any career workshops at your school or in your community.

6. In October (Sophomore or Junior Year) take the PLAN test and/or PSAT. **It is very important to note that the PSAT is used as the basis for selection for the National Merit Scholarship when you are a senior.** Do not be fooled by the word practice here.

In addition:_____

In addition:_____

In addition:_____

APPOINTMENTS

Date:_____ Time:_____ with_____

Re:_____

Date:_____ Time:_____ with_____

Re:_____

Date:_____ Time:_____ with_____

Re:_____

Date:_____ Time:_____ with_____

Re:_____

SOPHOMORE AND/OR JUNIOR YEAR
FALL

Date Scheduled   Date Completed

7. Continue to investigate career interests and various colleges.

8. Attend an ACT/SAT preparation class and/or review materials including computer programs provided by your counselor.

9. Prepare for the ACT or SAT by taking practice tests or use computer programs which utilize practice/sample questions.

10. Participate in any college recruiting sessions, career planning seminars etc.

11. Attend any college fairs available in your community.

12. Review your course load with the counselor and make sure you have not missed anything and are planning to take the remainder of any required courses.

13. Review your practice test scores with your counselor.

14. If applicable, talk to your counselor about Advance Placement Test and Achievement Tests.

In addition:_____

In addition:_____

In addition:_____

APPOINTMENTS

Date:_____ Time:_____ with_____

Re:_____

Date:_____ Time:_____ with_____

Re:_____

Date:_____ Time:_____ with_____

Re:_____

Date:_____ Time:_____ with_____

Re:_____

SOPHOMORE AND/OR JUNIOR YEAR SPRING

Date Scheduled   Date Completed

15. Pick up registration packets for ACT or SAT.

16. Take ACT or SAT test.

17. Set up meeting or attend necessary workshop on college application process.

18. Review your current transcripts for class rank and required courses.

19. Learn how to write a resume, get reference material and attend any workshops or classes. They should be offered at your school or community college.

20. Select potential college choices (6): Send for catalogs and videos, start to make visits (Summer is a good time for this). Talk to alumni. Review for cost, academic requirements and curriculum offered. Remember to match the college with the person.

21. Take ACT, SAT, Achievement tests if not already completed.

22. Continue to devote some thought to your career interests. Work on getting involved in extracurricular activities and part time jobs which interest you. Save any money you can.

In addition:_____

In addition:_____

In addition:_____

APPOINTMENTS

Date:_____ Time:_____ with_____

Re:_____

Date:_____ Time:_____ with_____

Re:_____

Date:_____ Time:_____ with_____

Re:_____

Date:_____ Time:_____ with_____

Re:_____

SENIOR YEAR
FALL

Date
Scheduled

Date
Completed

23. Review transcript and prepare resume. Make sure you are taking any required courses. Review your schedule with your counselor to make certain you are taking all courses required for admission.

24. Take ACT, SAT or Achievement Tests if not happy with previous scores.

25. Obtain and organize all application material from your 6 potential colleges. (Use the College Comparison Chart) Check deadlines and all information and fees required.

26. Ask for letters of recommendations from teachers. Keep lists of these teachers and be sure to check back with them to make sure they honored your request.

27. Begin to outline and prepare an essay for any applications that require an essay.

28. If you are going to take AP tests, let appropriate teacher know in January.

29. If applying for early decision, prepare application packet by the required deadline which is November in most instances.

30. Submit all college applications. This is best if done through your counselor. If you need help with your application fees, check with your counselor.

31. Apply for any scholarships & grants. Attend classes and workshops on financial aid. Do not forget about the FAF (Financial Aid Form), FFS (Family Financial Statement) or the FAFSA (Free Application for Federal Student Aid) **which is obtained from your counselor's office. This form must be submitted in January and is required in order to get any Pell Grants from the US Government.**

In addition:_____

In addition:_____

In addition:_____

APPOINTMENTS

Date:_____ Time:_____ with_____

Re:_____

Date:_____ Time:_____ with_____

Re:_____

Date:_____ Time:_____ with_____

Re:_____

SENIOR YEAR
SPRING

Date Scheduled | Date Completed |

32. Apply for financial aid. Begin process after January 1st and attend a financial aid workshop with your parents. Continue to apply for any scholarships.

33. Speak to your counselor on final college choice.

34. If the college you want to attend accepts you, send in necessary acceptance forms and pay any required deposits such as housing.

35. If first choice does not accept you, look at other ones that did and select one.

36. If other choice accepts you before you have heard from your first choice, then ask for extension on your deposit.

37. If no choices accept you, then don't go to college. Just kidding. Select another choice and repeat the application process.

38. Take AP 's if necessary.

39. Review college catalog and discuss with your counselor and parents course selections.

40. Party and work all summer.

In addition:_____

In addition:_____

In addition:_____

APPOINTMENTS

Date:_____ Time:_____ with_____

Re:_____

Date:_____ Time:_____ with_____

Re:_____

Date:_____ Time:_____ with_____

Re:_____

Date:_____ Time:_____ with_____

Re:_____

Hey, What About. . . ?

Students use the "Hey What About Section" to write down any additional questions you may have after you read each chapter.

More Stuff to Worry About

Counselors use the "More Stuff To Worry About" section to add additional material, presentation information, handouts or other relevant thoughts about each chapter.

☐ Read it. . . _____

_____

_____

☐ Check It Out. . . _____

_____

_____

☐ Fill It Out. . . _____

_____

_____

☐ Think About It. . . _____

_____

_____

NOTES

Chapter 2

DEVELOPING AN EXTREMELY COOL TRANSCRIPT AND RESUME

The process of developing an extremely cool transcript and resume should not, by any means, be a painful, rigidly controlled, predetermined process, which will be directed, at any cost, to creating an A student, all-star athlete, student body president, science fair award recipient, or Ken and Barbie clones (yes, the dolls, which are not even anatomically correct). A student should simply try to do his or her best at everything they do and enjoy doing it.

Your classes, grades, class ranking, attendance and disciplinary records are definitely important. Taking more challenging classes in high school can only help when confronted with more difficult courses in college. Believe me, the classes do not get any easier in college. The harder you are on yourself with challenging classes in high school, the easier colleges will be on analyzing your transcript. Give yourself a fair shot at the university you want by maintaining a good attendance record and don't play around too much. The easier you make life for your teachers the more likely you are to have a few who will write you letters of recommendation. As you know, there is plenty of time to mess around outside of school.

Definitely try to participate in at least one extracurricular activity, either Sports, Band, Debate/Speech, Theater or the School Newspaper. If none of these interests you, almost any hobby, past time or job can be turned into a resume builder. If you like music, start a band or work at a record shop. If you like to build things or fix cars, get a job as a carpenter or mechanics apprentice. Maybe you like animals, so you can get a job as a vet's assistant, work at the zoo or get a job at a dog kennel. Ask your parents and friends about people they know who are in a business you are interested in, and see if they will hire you part-time. If no paid positions are available, ask if an internship would be possible. If you can spare the time and can afford not to get paid for awhile, this will usually turn into a paid position, if you do a good job. An internship will definitely result in some type of skill training or experience.

Also look into some volunteer work with a needy organization or your church, even if it is only one day a month. This kind of selfless work is not only good for you, but it looks great on a resume and contributes greatly to whatever organization you are helping. In addition, helping those less fortunate than yourself will always help you keep things in perspective in your own life. Your school might have a Social Awareness class whereby you do volunteer work for the needy and get class credits. Take advantage of this opportunity if it is available. (See Chapter 10: On Survival)

All the above activities are ideas to improve yourself and to make your transcript and resume look better to a college admissions office. Keep in mind, transcripts and resumes are only a reflection of you on a piece of paper. So think about what you would like to see, and what you want other people to see when they look at your reflection.

Remember, while participating in any of life's activities, put the most you can into everything you do!! There are two old sayings that when translated into the 20th century read "Don't torch any bridges" and "Treat others like you would want to be treated" Do your best at everything you do, whether it is washing dishes, stocking groceries or flipping burgers. And always treat other people just like you would want to be treated.

All colleges have minimum academic requirements. Check with your guidance counselor as early as possible to be sure you are taking all the required courses necessary for college admission and are meeting the grade requirements. In addition, check your potential colleges academic requirements and see if you qualify. You can use the High School Course Check Up, College Requirement Chart and the Resume Builder below to see where you stand.

HIGH SCHOOL COURSE CHECK UP

What I have taken so far and will take in the future:

9TH GRADE

COURSE TITLE	CREDITS	COURSE TITLE	CREDITS
TOTALS			

10TH GRADE

COURSE TITLE	CREDITS	COURSE TITLE	CREDITS
TOTALS			

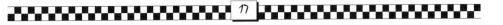

HIGH SCHOOL COURSE CHECK UP CONTINUED...

	COURSE TITLE	CREDITS	COURSE TITLE	CREDITS
11TH GRADE				
	TOTAL			

	COURSE TITLE	CREDITS	COURSE TITLE	CREDITS
12TH GRADE				
	TOTAL			

	COURSE TITLE	CREDITS	COURSE TITLE	CREDITS
STILL NEED/WANT TO TAKE				

COLLEGE CREDIT REQUIREMENTS

What my college choices require me to have taken:

CREDITS	COLLEGE #1	COLLEGE #2
Name of College:		
English:		
Math:		
Sciences:		
Social Sciences:		
Foreign Language:		
Other:		
(P.E., Computer, Electives)		
Total		

CREDITS	COLLEGE #3	COLLEGE #4
Name of College:		
English:		
Math:		
Sciences:		
Social Sciences:		
Foreign Language:		
Other:		
(P.E., Computer, Electives)		
Total		

CREDITS	COLLEGE #5	COLLEGE #6
Name of College:		
English:		
Math:		
Sciences:		
Social Sciences:		
Foreign Language:		
Other:		
(P.E., Computer, Electives)		
Total		

RESUME BUILDERS

Clubs & Organizations I belong to:

NAME OF CLUB/ORGANIZATION	POSITIONS HELD	YEARS INVOLVED
SPORTS:		

AWARDS:

HOBBIES:

TRAVEL:

Jobs Held:

EMPLOYER	POSITION	HOURS	DATES

People who would write letters of recommendations for me besides me:

SCHOOL PERSONNEL/EMPLOYERS/PERSONAL	PHONE

People who would not write letters of recommendations for me and that I will take off my Christmas card list and taunt at every opportunity.

Remember: It is never too late to take study courses such as Speed Reading or Study Skills Improvement Courses. It is never too late and it should be an ongoing process to explore potential career options. Try to work in any field that might interest you. How else are you really going to know if you are suited for and would enjoy a particular profession? How are you going to know if you would like to be restaurant manager unless you have worked in a restaurant as a waitress or waiter? Maybe you want to be a jet pilot, but you projectile puke when you fly in planes or go on roller coasters. Maybe you want to be a rock star, but have not yet sung in the school choir or played an instrument in the band. Now is the time to check it out and explore any of your interests through participating in them as jobs or even hobbies. This allows you to narrow down what you would truly like to "be when you grow up". (See Chapter 7: Majors)

Remember, always work to improve yourself. Steady improvement throughout your high school years is a good sign to college admission offices. Let's take some time to list your goals and what you are going to do to achieve them.

GOALS	STEPS TO ACHIEVE THEM
1	
2	
3	
4	
5	
6	

Hey, What About. . . ?

More Stuff to Worry About

☐ Read it. . . _____

_____

_____

☐ Check It Out. . . _____

_____

_____

☐ Fill It Out. . . _____

_____

_____

☐ Think About It. . . _____

_____

_____

NOTES

Chapter 3

SO WHERE
ARE YOU GOING?

Selecting a college or university may seem like a monstrous task. I mean there are two year, four-year, out-of-state, in-state, private, public, small, large, schools with great football teams, schools with no football teams, expensive, and, well, really expensive schools. How do you decide which one is right for you? Well, it is easy. **First decide what you want and then find the schools that have it and would want you.**

You can make your choice much easier by not studying, not working, not being involved in extracurricular activities or by dropping out of high school. This would limit the number of colleges that would accept you. Some colleges and universities have strict requirements for admission, both academic and extracurricular. So I hope you paid attention while you read "Developing an extremely cool transcript and resume" because it makes a difference.

So what do you want? To be the next Spike Lee or Madonna? Maybe Bill Clinton or a Maria Shriver? Would you like to be a space shuttle astronaut, bike shop owner, shark researcher, politician, rock video producer or an attorney? Or do you have simpler, more earthly ambitions, like just being able to find someone to drive this Friday night? You don't know? Well that's typical! Here, I'll make it easy on you. Just answer these three questions:

First: Why do you want to go to college?

☐ To study and get into graduate school . . .

☐ To play a sport . . .

☐ Because my parents want me to . . .

☐ Because of all the wild parties I've heard about . . .

☐ To prepare me for the career I selected which is _____.

☐ To achieve a higher level of education which would benefit myself and society . . .? Yeah right!

☐ To help me decide what career I want . . .

☐ To move away from home . . .

☐ Because all my friends are . . .

☐ I have no clue . . .

Now list any other reasons you have for wanting to go to college, not the reasons you think you are supposed to have, but your real thoughts:

1. _____

2. _____

3. _____

4. _____

Second: Where do you think you would like to go to college?

☐ Big school...

☐ Small school...

☐ Big school in a small town...

☐ Small school in a big town...

☐ In-State

☐ Out-of-State

☐ In the mountains

☐ On the ocean

☐ In the city

☐ In the country

Name:_____

Name:_____

Name:_____

Name:_____

Name:_____

Name:_____

Third: Are you qualified academically and financially?

I have a pretty good transcript consisting
of challenging courses   ☐ Yes ☐ No ☐ Maybe So

I have participated in various extracurricular
activities and have held jobs   ☐ Yes ☐ No ☐ Maybe So

My GPA is_____

My class rank is _____

My SAT score is_____.

My ACT score is_____.

My ACH scores are____,_____,_____.

My parents are cool on me going to
wherever I can get in   ☐ Yes ☐ No ☐ Maybe So

I think I am qualified for a scholarship   ☐ Yes ☐ No ☐ Maybe So

As it stands now, I can afford $ /year for college

I think I can qualify for financial aid   ☐ Yes ☐ No ☐ Maybe So

After you have devoted some thought to the above three questions, you are ready to check with your counselor or local library and have them direct you to some good reference books and software which list different college profiles. These publications, along with various colleges catalogs are good starting points. You may write to any college you choose for their catalog if your counselor does not have a copy. Simply write a letter stating you are interested in attending their college and would like a catalog and any other information on attending their school. When reviewing this information be sure and check carefully tuition and the cost for room and board. Compare your potential college's academic programs and see which one offers the most.

Use the College Choice Comparison Chart to compare information on your choices. As you collect information from your visits to colleges, college recruiting visits to your high school, reference books or college catalogs, add notes and fill in your chart. Enter your schools in the order of preference. Number one is your first choice, number 2 is your second, so on and so on.

College Comparison Chart	COLLEGE #1	COLLEGE #2
Name:		
Location:		
SAT/ACT Scores requirement:		
GPA requirements:		
Admission Options w/dates: (Regular, Early Decision, Early Action, Rolling)		
Received application packet:	☐ Yes ☐ No	☐ Yes ☐ No
Deposits Required & Is It Refundable?:		
Do I meet the academic requirements?:	☐ Yes ☐ No	☐ Yes ☐ No
Tuition/year:	$	$
Room & Board:	$	$
Travel Costs:	$	$
Has the major I want?:		
Academically known for:		
Extracurricularly known for:		
Prominent Alumni: Good Contacts		
Student/Teacher Ratio: Average Class Size		
Number of Students Enrolled: Male/Female	☐ Male ☐ Female	☐ Male ☐ Female
Ethnically diverse:		
% of students admitted to graduate schools:		

College Comparison Chart	COLLEGE #1	COLLEGE #2
Potential Scholarships and or aid for me: See also Chapter 4		
Sports: Intramural and intercollegiate available:		
Academic Support Services: Y/N (Counseling, Tutors)	☐ Yes ☐ No	☐ Yes ☐ No
Dorms/Frats/Sororities:		
Off Campus Housing/ Safe Neighborhood:		
Transportation required: Y/N (Bikes or Cars or Dog sleds)	☐ Yes ☐ No	☐ Yes ☐ No
Handicap Access to all facilities: Y/N	☐ Yes ☐ No	☐ Yes ☐ No
Cafeteria/ Local Food Spots:		
Internships & overseas study available:		
College job opportunities:		
Rules & Regulations: (Visitation, Drinking)		
Use of campus computer labs:		
What I have heard: (Can surf here - Good parties here)		

College Comparison Chart	COLLEGE #3	COLLEGE #4
Name:		
Location:		
SAT/ACT Scores requirement:		
GPA requirements:		
Admission Options w/dates: (Regular, Early Decision, Early Action, Rolling)		
Received application packet:	☐ Yes ☐ No	☐ Yes ☐ No
Deposits Required & Is It Refundable?:		
Do I meet the academic requirements?:	☐ Yes ☐ No	☐ Yes ☐ No
Tuition/year:	$	$
Room & Board:	$	$
Travel Costs:	$	$
Has the major I want?:		
Academically known for:		
Extracurricularly known for:		
Prominent Alumni: Good Contacts		
Student/Teacher Ratio: Average Class Size		
Number of Students Enrolled: Male/Female	☐ Male ☐ Female	☐ Male ☐ Female
Ethnically diverse:		
% of students admitted to graduate schools:		

College Comparison Chart	COLLEGE #3	COLLEGE #4
Potential Scholarships and or aid for me: See also Chapter 4		
Sports: Intramural and intercollegiate available:		
Academic Support Services: Y/N (Counseling, Tutors)	☐ Yes ☐ No	☐ Yes ☐ No
Dorms/Frats/Sororities:		
Off Campus Housing/ Safe Neighborhood:		
Transportation required: Y/N (Bikes or Cars or Dog sleds)	☐ Yes ☐ No	☐ Yes ☐ No
Handicap Access to all facilities: Y/N	☐ Yes ☐ No	☐ Yes ☐ No
Cafeteria/ Local Food Spots:		
Internships & overseas study available:		
College job opportunities:		
Rules & Regulations: (Visitation, Drinking)		
Use of campus computer labs:		
What I have heard: (Can surf here - Good parties here)		

College Comparison Chart	COLLEGE #5	COLLEGE #6
Name:		
Location:		
SAT/ACT Scores requirement:		
GPA requirements:		
Admission Options w/dates: (Regular, Early Decision, Early Action, Rolling)		
Received application packet:	☐ Yes ☐ No	☐ Yes ☐ No
Deposits Required & Is It Refundable?:		
Do I meet the academic requirements?:	☐ Yes ☐ No	☐ Yes ☐ No
Tuition/year:	$	$
Room & Board:	$	$
Travel Costs:	$	$
Has the major I want?:		
Academically known for:		
Extracurricularly known for:		
Prominent Alumni: Good Contacts		
Student/Teacher Ratio: Average Class Size		
Number of Students Enrolled: Male/Female	☐ Male ☐ Female	☐ Male ☐ Female
Ethnically diverse:		
% of students admitted to graduate schools:		

College Comparison Chart	COLLEGE #5	COLLEGE #6
Potential Scholarships and or aid for me: See also Chapter 4		
Sports: Intramural and intercollegiate available:		
Academic Support Services: Y/N (Counseling, Tutors)	☐ Yes ☐ No	☐ Yes ☐ No
Dorms/Frats/Sororities:		
Off Campus Housing/ Safe Neighborhood:		
Transportation required: Y/N (Bikes or Cars or Dog sleds)	☐ Yes ☐ No	☐ Yes ☐ No
Handicap Access to all facilities: Y/N	☐ Yes ☐ No	☐ Yes ☐ No
Cafeteria/ Local Food Spots:		
Internships & overseas study available:		
College job opportunities:		
Rules & Regulations: (Visitation, Drinking)		
Use of campus computer labs:		
What I have heard: (Can surf here - Good parties here)		

By reviewing this information you will be able to compare your six potential college choices and narrow down the schools you are interested in most. Obviously, only schools you can afford should be considered, right? Not necessarily. Do not give up on schools that appear too expensive until you have exhausted all possible scholarships and financial aid considerations. Once you see if a financial aid package is offered to you, then you will be able to determine if you can afford a particular school. You should choose at least six schools you would like to attend, however, feel free to use the previous chart to compare as many as you like.

A personal visit is a good idea if possible. Wait, let me say that another way. A personal visit is highly, highly recommended! By visiting your potential college(s) before applying, you can see things for yourself. Stay with some friends who go there. Check out the surrounding neighborhoods, campus, gym, cafeteria, bulletin boards, sit in on classes, check the school paper, libraries, dorm rooms, city or town where the college is located. Talk to professors and students currently in your major. Check the rules of living in the dorms and general campus regulations. Talk to both first year students and upper classmen about the school. If you cannot pay a personal visit to your potential college, then get a 4D ultraanimational virtual reality video brain insert where you can actually go to the college in your mind without physically being there. Actually I am not sure if these exist yet, in any case, most colleges have videos which they will send you free. It's the next best thing to being there.

A student's primary reason for attending a particular college should center around the fact that a potential college choice offers the academic program the student wants to pursue. There are, however, other reasons that should be weighed. There are many schools which offer business majors or Pre-Med, so after you determine a choice has your desired academic program, what are some of the other considerations?

Well, definitely a major factor in the college selection process is whether to attend a college close to home or far away, in-state versus out-of-state. Attending a school that is out-of-state can be a great learning experience in addition to the normal classroom learning. Meeting people from all over the country and experiencing a diverse environment from the one in which you grew up can be a real kick!

Although the thought of leaving your hometown and your old friends might make you nervous and apprehensive, it has some definite advantages. There might be things about yourself you always wanted to change, but, due to stereotypes, or what your friends think of you, you have really not had the opportunity to break out of certain behaviors. These behaviors or roles usually exist in high school. Maybe you wanted to party less, get in good shape, be more social, really concentrate on school, start painting or taking dance. Any of these might represent something you wanted to pursue, but did not, for whatever reasons. It is easier when you are away from old surroundings, and peers with expectations, to make these changes. When you tell your new college friends you are going to the gym or jogging, they do not consider this strange and bother you as to why you don't just go throw a frisbee or go to a movie.

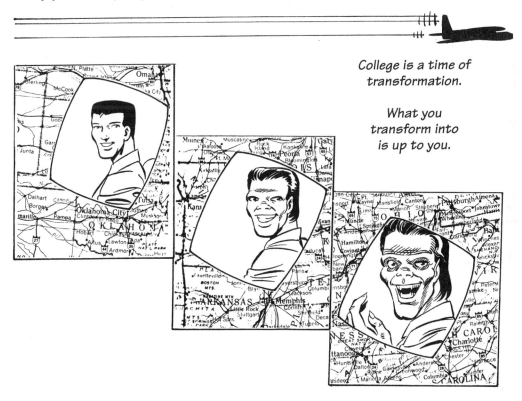

College is a time of transformation.

What you transform into is up to you.

Whether or not to attend a large or small college is also a factor. Large schools have tremendous extracurricular opportunities, such as clubs and intercollegiate sports, while small schools boast about small class sizes and friendlier campuses. Look at these **Rate Master Tables** for assessing your desire to attend a Small School vs. Large School and for Going Away From Home vs. Staying Close To Home. Rate items which are important to you and see what you might prefer.

SMALL SCHOOL VS. LARGE SCHOOL

	COULD CARE LESS ... MASSIVELY IMPORTANT				
Large intercollegiate sports programs:	1	2	3	4	5
Active large scale social scenes:	1	2	3	4	5
Nightly social events:	1	2	3	4	5
Fraternities & Sororities:	1	2	3	4	5
Multitude of clubs & organizations:	1	2	3	4	5
Academic resources, labs & research centers:	1	2	3	4	5
Cultural Diversity:	1	2	3	4	5
Smaller Class size:	5	4	3	2	1
Waiting in lines:	5	4	3	2	1
Add responses	SCORE= _____				

GOING AWAY FROM HOME VS. STAYING CLOSE TO HOME

	NOT A PROBLEM .... A MAJOR PROBLEM				
Being away from parents:	1	2	3	4	5
Leaving hometown:	1	2	3	4	5
Not being around old friends regularly:	1	2	3	4	5
Writing letters:	1	2	3	4	5
Meeting new people:	1	2	3	4	5
Expanding my horizons:	1	2	3	4	5
Adjusting to new circumstances:	1	2	3	4	5
Being on my own:	1	2	3	4	5
Add responses	SCORE= _____				

If you received a 30 or higher on the Small School vs. Large School **Rate Master** then you should think seriously about attending a larger university. If you received a 15 or less then you should think about attending a smaller college. If you received something in between, then, you should just plain think.

If you received a 27 or higher on the Going Away vs. Staying Close to Home **Rate Master** then you should think seriously about attending a school close to home. If you received a 14 or less then you should think about going to school farther away. If you received something in between, then you should just plain think.

Actually you might be able to get some of the benefits of both by attending a small college in a large city or a large college in a small town. If the school offers what you need academically, then you might benefit from a more convenient campus set-up, better class size and generally all the benefits of a smaller school, while not foregoing any of the cultural benefits of a large city such as professional sporting events, theater and general cosmopolitan lifestyle. Keep in mind, although larger universities usually have a wider spectrum of party activities, there are definitely some small colleges around the nation that party just as much, if not more than, big schools.

Make sure you talk to current students at each of your potential colleges, both freshmen and upperclassmen. Note their comments in the "What have I heard" section of your CCC.

Many colleges will come to your school to recruit students. Attend as many presentations as possible. Write down a list of important questions you want to ask before you go to the presentations. Keep in mind these people are there to recruit you, so ask tough questions and don't settle for vague answers. In addition, do not take their word as final, without checking first with other less biased sources.

One final note, if you decide to transfer from one college to another, make sure you follow the golden rule: Get the acceptance of course credits which are transferable in writing from your new college before you transfer.

COLLEGE RECRUITMENT PRESENTATIONS

Remember before the presentations, prepare questions you want to ask the recruiters. Bring this book to take notes in or at least a copy of the College Comparison Chart.

COLLEGE	DATE	TIME	PLACE

COLLEGE VISITS PLANNED

COLLEGE	DATE	TIME	CONTACT

Hey, What About. . . ?

More Stuff to Worry About

☐ Read it. . . _____

_____

_____

☐ Check It Out. . . _____

_____

_____

☐ Fill It Out. . . _____

_____

_____

☐ Think About It. . . _____

_____

_____

NOTES

Chapter 4

HOW YA GONNA
PAY FOR IT?

So how are you going to pay for college, huh? huh? Did you ever in your life, for one lousy stinking minute, think about how you are going to pay for it huh...huh . . . aaaaaaaahhhhhhhhhhhh!!!!!!!!!!

This is obviously one of the more important considerations about going to college. If you cannot afford a particular school, then you simply cannot attend it, right? The average, public, four year college costs approximately $7,500 per year. Private and Ivy League schools can run as high as $24,000 per year. But, before you panic, make sure you investigate all financial aid programs, such as potential job opportunities, work study programs and all scholarships and grants. There are some excellent reference books available from your library and through your guidance counselors which deal exclusively with financial aid. Make sure you check into these!!

Unfortunately, in regards to a savings plan, outlining a college investment plan to begin your junior or senior year in high school is not going to pay for your four years of college. However, keep in mind every little bit helps. See Chapter 9 for some financial survival tips and check out any of the sources your counselor recommends. Remember, any amount of money will help pay for books, tuition, expenses and an occasional pizza. So get off your butt and get a part time job, or at least be prepared to work if time permits or lack of money demands it.

The first thing you need to do is find out how much your potential colleges cost. Make sure you add up all the costs. Estimate what one year would cost and start to plan accordingly. Hopefully you have saved for college since you were four years old and now have ample cash to pay for school plus a few Spring Break trips. Yeah right!

ESTIMATED ANNUAL COLLEGE COST:

School Name						
Tuition =						
Lab & Other Fees=						
Room & Board =						
Travel =						
Books & School Supplies =						
Clothes =						
Personal =						
Medical =						
Savings =						
Insurances =						
Phone Bills =						
Party Funds (ooo's) =						
Auto =						
Bicycle =						
Furniture &Fixtures =						
Miscellaneous =						
TOTAL PER YEAR (Add columns)	$	$	$	$	$	$

Note: Examine these costs for a four year period in order to plan effectively for the financial requirements of your college education. Use this chart before the beginning of each school year to help plan your budget. Don't forget to add in the cost of living index from year to year. Simply multiple your total by .08 and add that number to your total.

Now that you have estimated how much college is going to cost you, let us see how much you have. Zero, zilch, goose egg, -0-, nada, ninguno, nothing! O.K. that was easy.

WHAT YOU HAVE AND WHAT YOU NEED:

School Name						
Total College Costs (from previous page)	$	$	$	$	$	$
Student Contribution:						
Birth to date Savings +						
Estimated savings from jobs held until start of freshman year +						
Parental Contribution:						
Parents +						
Relatives +						
Lotto winnings! +						
Student and Parent Contribution Totals:						
Total:	$	$	$	$	$	$
Potential financial need (College Costs - Student Contribution and Parent's Contribution) =						
Total:	$	$	$	$	$	$

It is important to note that by applying for financial aid, you are allowing yourself the opportunity to qualify for federal and state grants and low interest loans such as the Perkins or Stafford loans. In addition, college work study programs are selected based on financial need. Make certain you fill out a need analysis form (FAF, FFS, FAFSA) prior to your application deadlines.

If you have taken advantage of the opportunities available in your high school, chances are you can qualify for various college scholarships that are available today. Review your academic history with your counselor and see if a potential scholarship search would be worthwhile. If you managed to maintain an above average GPA in school, received SAT or ACT scores above the national average, have kept yourself busy enough to have an "extremely cool" resume, then you should apply for every scholarship whose criteria you meet. How do you find out about these scholarships?

1st Check to see which scholarships your counselor knows about and research them, based on the discussion you have already had regarding your academic history. (Right, you already spoke to your counselor!!?)

2nd Check to see which merit scholarships your potential colleges offer. You know how to use a phone, don't you? This information should be available in any college introduction packet, usually in the college catalog.

3rd Check out any reference books and computer programs recommended by your counselor for scholarship information. There are some very useful books dedicated solely to financing college, student loans, grants and scholarships. **Make sure the edition you buy, borrow or check-out is for the current year.**

You should also follow these steps when searching for other sources of financial aid such as grants or loans. After a thorough search of potential scholarships, grants and loans, it is wise to apply for everything under the sun. If you feel you potentially could qualify for a grant or aid package, then take the time and apply fur it ("fur" is country for "for"). Of course, if your are a white male from an upper class family who flunked history in high school, you really need not bother to apply for the minority girls historical valedictorian college grant. But there are so many available, you really should apply for as many as possible. You would be surprised at the number of scholarships, grants and potential loan dollars which go unused every year. Don't forget ROTC or other military financial opportunities if you are interested in serving in the military. In addition, don't forget to check out your parents, Rotary clubs, Eagles or any other civic organizations that might be a source of funds. Your counselor should be able to give you the scoops on these. Remember, loans need to be paid back while scholarships and grants do not! Do not forget to fill out the FAF, FFS or FAFSA. You can get these, as well as assistance in filling them out correctly, from your counselor's office.

POTENTIAL LOANS, GRANTS AND/OR SCHOLARSHIPS TO APPLY FOR:

LOANS:

BANKS OR ORGANIZATIONS	REPAYMENT TERM & INTEREST	FORMS/INFORMATION REQUIRED & SUBMITTED	$AMOUNT	DEADLINE

SCHOLARSHIPS & GRANTS:

SCHOOL OR ORGANIZATION	QUALIFICATIONS	$AMOUNT	RENEWAL REQUIREMENTS	APPLICATION DEADLINE	FORMS/INFO. REQUIRED & SUBMITTED

In addition to exploring various types of financial aid, be sure to explore part time jobs while you are in school and full time jobs for the summer. Get a paper from your college town and check through the classified section. Also, check into work study programs, which are part of financial aid packages. Students must qualify for this program which hires them for jobs available right on campus.

POTENTIAL PART TIME JOBS

BUSINESS/LOCATION				
1st	2nd	3rd	4th	5th
PHONE#				
CONTACT				
HOURS				
PAY				
CALLED / SENT RESUME				
INTERVIEW / TIME AND DATE				

Hey, What About. . . ?

More Stuff to Worry About

☐ Read it. . . _____
_____
_____

☐ Check It Out. . . _____
_____
_____

☐ Fill It Out. . . _____
_____
_____

☐ Think About It. . . _____
_____
_____

NOTES

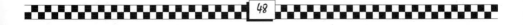

Chapter 5

TESTS YOU MUST TAKE TO GET IN

ACT, SAT, ACH, OHNO!!

What is going on? Not only do you have tests in all your classes in high school, in addition, now you have to take more tests, to see if you learned anything by taking all those other tests, to see if you can go to another place which will make you take even more tests! That made about as much sense as: (Fill in your own please)._____

_____

Although the thought of more tests might make you sick, look on the bright side. You probably have already prepared for them simply by attending your high school classes and doing your best. However, to give you the added edge and to help familiarize yourself with the testing methods, it is suggested you take a practice test and follow your counselors recommendations on any test preparation activities. Each college has its own requirement as to what test you need for admission, so check with your counselor and/or the catalogs and jot it down on your Application Deadlines and Requirements Chart found in Chapter 6.

TEST PREPARATION ACTIVITIES		
What	When	Where

"So go ahead, make my day and tell me about more tests I have to take."

O.K. I will.

(Some sections excerpted from the College Entrance Examination Board Booklets Copyright 1991)

PLAN+ is a four part exam testing the following areas:

1. Writing Skills
2. Mathematics Test
3. Reading Test
4. Science Reasoning Test

The test is designed to measure a student's skill and knowledge already acquired in the early years of high school. Students are given one hour and fifty minutes to complete the four sections. The test sections are scored individually from 1-32. A composite score average of all four sections is taken. In addition, there are other scores provided to help assess a student's writing and math skills. There is an additional section which will help a student look at potential career interests. The PLAN is a great way for students to see where they are and to help prepare them for the ACT. Highly recommended!

PSAT/NMSQT (Preliminary Scholastic Aptitude Test/National Merit Scholarship Qualifying Test)

is a test that measures verbal and math reasoning abilities important for academic success in college. Multiple choice, sentence completion and constructing answers in the math section are all part of the new PSAT/NMSQT. Calculators are allowed. The sections covered are outlined below under SAT-I. **This test is extremely important!!! The PSAT/NMSQT gives students practice for the SAT-I and enables students to be considered for certain scholarships, especially the National Merit Scholarships.**

SAT-I (The Scholastic Aptitude Test) is a three hour plus aptitude test consisting of two sections. The Verbal Reasoning section tests the student's critical reading abilities and the Mathematical Reasoning section tests the student's problem solving abilities which are important for college success.

1. Verbal Section: 70-85 questions; Test time=75-80 minutes.
   a. Sentence Completion: 20-25 questions
   b. Analogies: 15-20 questions
   c. Critical Reading: 30-40 questions; 4 different passages
      (Humanities, Social Sciences, Natural Sciences and Narrative)
   •Antonyms are no longer included in the new SAT-I.

2. Mathematics Section: 60 questions; Test time=70-75 minutes.
   a. Student Produced Responses: 10 questions
   b. Quantitative Comparisons: 15 questions
   c. Regular Mathematics: 35 multiple choice questions
   •Calculators are allowed and test contains new questions that require students to produce their own answers, not just select multiple choice alternatives.

The test sections are scored individually from 200-800, Verbal and Math separately. Potential Scholarship score is 1200 and above. There is a slight penalty for guessing, so if you run out of time, "well thought out bombs away"!!! The test is taken primarily for admissions. For more information ask your counselor or call the SAT-I College Board Office at 212-713-8175.

ACT (American College Test) is a four part test consisting of the following sections:

1. English: 45 minutes to complete 75 items.
2. Mathematics Test: 60 minutes to complete 60 items.
3. Reading Test: 35 minutes to complete 40 items.
4. Science Reasoning Test: 35 minutes to complete 40 items.

The test sections are scored individually from 1-36. A composite score average of all four sections is taken. The national composite average score is around 20. Potential Scholarship scores are 28-35. Remember, there is no penalty for guessing. So if you start to run out of time,"bombs away"!!! For more information ask your counselor or call the ACT National Office at 319-337-1270.

It is recommended you take the ACT or SAT-I in the spring of your junior year. If you are not happy with your scores, you can retake the test at the beginning of your senior year.

ACH (Achievement Tests) are a multiple choice format which tests the student's achievement in a specific subject. They are scored individually from 200-800. There are ACH tests for the following subjects:

1. English Composition
2. Biology
3. Chemistry
4. Physics
5. Math: Level I & II
6. French, Spanish, German, Latin, Hebrew, Italian
7. American History
8. European History
9. Literature

You should take a particular ACH test after you have completed the particular course in high school. They are usually taken for placement. If you feel particularly strong in a subject, it is highly recommended that you take the ACH test for that subject.

Besides paying attention to your regular classes and following your counselor's advice as far as practice tests, etc. make sure you get a good nights sleep before you take any of the above tests, and most of all relax while taking the test.

POSSIBLE TEST DATES:

TEST	REGISTRATION/ DEADLINE	FEES:	TIME:	DATE:	PLACE

COLLEGE ADMISSION REQUIREMENTS:
(minimum scores accepted)

	MY SCORE	COLLEGE	COLLEGE	COLLEGE	COLLEGE	COLLEGE	COLLEGE
ACT							
COM-POSITE							
SAT:							
VERBAL							
MATH							

Hey, What About. . . ?

More Stuff to Worry About

❑ Read it. . . _____

_____

_____

❑ Check It Out. . . _____

_____

_____

❑ Fill It Out. . . _____

_____

_____

❑ Think About It. . . _____

_____

_____

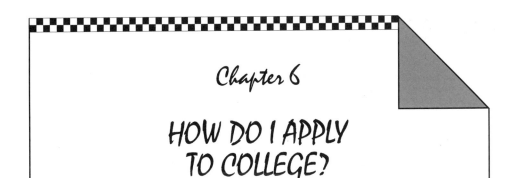

Chapter 6

HOW DO I APPLY TO COLLEGE?

Forms, Letters of Recommendations, Essays, Interviews

There really is not much to the application process, you just "do it" and "do it" by the deadline given in the college catalog! Each college has its own admissions requirements which are outlined in the school's catalog along with any necessary forms. Most colleges require some combination of the below listed packet be sent when applying. Private colleges usually require 1-6 while public universities usually do not require 4,5 or 6.

1. Application Forms

2. Admission Test Scores (sent directly on your request from the testing agency)

3. High School Transcripts (provided by your high school)

4. Letters of Recommendation

5. Essay (if applicable)

6. Interview (if applicable)

The college catalog will also give you important information on curriculum offered, financial aid, housing, academic requirements and other important admissions information. You have already noted some important information regarding admissions criteria and other relevant data in your College Comparison Chart and College Course/Credit Requirements Check Up. Now, you should double check your application deadlines and requirements for your six potential colleges.

Mark down a date at least 5 weeks before the actual deadline given. Make sure you have all your application packet together and proofed and to your counselors office by that time.

APPLICATIONS DEADLINES AND REQUIREMENTS:

COLLEGE	APPLICATION DEADLINES	MY DEADLINE	ESSAY Y/N	INTERVIEW Y/N & DATE	SAT/ACT Y/N SUBMITTED
1					
2					
3					
4					
5					
6					

When preparing your application remember the following:

1. Read each application very carefully and follow all instructions exactly.

2. Have someone else proofread your application.

3. Ask your counselor any questions you have regarding the application.

4. Be sure to sign the form & include any fees or deposits.

5. **Maintain copies of everything you send.**

6. Send the application through your counselor's office (transcripts are added to the packet at this time.)

Letters of Recommendation:

Hopefully, up to this point in your high school career, you have not been a jerk to every single teacher or counselor you have ever met. Ideally, there are one or two you feel confident about asking for a letter of recommendation. If not, just make up your own and sign the principal's name to it. Yeah, that's the ticket. Actually that would be dishonest and illegal. In addition, a college might get a little suspicious when they see phrases like "world's greatest student and friend to the world, the most knock-out hot dynamite stick gorgeous senior, or sure to be the next Albert Einstein".

If you have not become personal friends with any teachers, counselors or coaches by now, you should really try. Not to just get a letter of recommendation out of them, but to learn from them and their personal experiences, and to form a genuine friendship. Preferably, find someone who knows you outside the classroom. As you know, there is a whole different you outside those four walls and a chalk board. Just because you don't understand the Periodic Table of Elements or know who signed the Treaty of Versailles, does not make you a worthless person. In my opinion, the Periodic Table of Elements is overrated. They should shorten it to carbonated water, fructose, sucrose, phosphoric acid, caffeine, niacin, thiamine, riboflavin, enriched flour, cheese, tomato paste, garlic and onions, which are basically the chemical components of pop and pizza. Your transcript will speak of your academic abilities, let the letters of recommendation speak for the other side of you.

When approaching people for letters of recommendation, do it early and give them a copy of your resume to help them. Also, let them know the deadline and pay them a visit about a week before it is due. Also check back with them to make sure they have been sent. And don't forget to thank them.

Some colleges require submitting a written essay with your application. An essay gives you the opportunity to illustrate your positive attributes which the rest of the application material does not always bring out. It allows a college to see if you can write coherently. Select a topic which is very personal to you and is easy, yet meaningful, to write about. Definitely spend some time on this and have your English teacher and several other people proofread it.

LETTERS OF RECOMMENDATIONS:

	WHO TO ASK	DATE DUE	REMINDED THEM
1			
2			
3			
4			
5			

Some colleges are going to require an interview as part of the application process. If you have never been through an interview of any kind, it is a good idea to conduct a few practice interviews with willing family members, counselors, teachers or friends. Have them ask you questions such as, "Why do you want to go to Hanging with Higher Education U?," or "What is one of your favorite classes and why?". In addition, you should practice asking questions too, and **not** questions like, "Will I have to study much if I go to college?" or "What sorority has the best keggers"?

After you are accepted to a particular college, you will receive an information packet containing preregistration forms, housing information (roommate questionnaire, dorm selection) and other general information such as course book and college calendar. Fill out all forms carefully and submit them as soon as possible.

Try not to take any summer school before your freshman year, enjoy the summer and your friends. If you want to do something take a reading comprehension course, memory or study course. At least try to read a book or four over the summer. Do not forget to have an ample abundance of ambitious amusement (fun), during your last summer before college.

CLASSES, MEETINGS OR PRESENTATIONS TO ATTEND REGARDING APPLICATION PROCESS:

TOPIC:	TIME:	DATE:	PLACE:

Double check! Do you have your "word that I am not supposed to use that begins with an "S" and contains an "h" and also an "i" and ends with a "t" together:

	Yes	No	Date Scheduled	Date Completed	Get From:
Initial meeting with counselor on college.	☐	☐			
Checked to see that academic requirements are being met.	☐	☐			
Learned how to write a resume.	☐	☐			
Selected six potential colleges.	☐	☐			
Secured all potential choices application packets.	☐	☐			
Completed College Comparison Chart.	☐	☐			
Researched financial aid and scholarships.	☐	☐			
Completed college costs analysis in Chapter 4.	☐	☐			
Taken ACT/SAT practice tests.	☐	☐			
Registered for ACT/SAT.	☐	☐			
Completed ACT/SAT/ACH tests.	☐	☐			
Submitted list of schools to send tests scores to.	☐	☐			
Asked for letters of recommendation.	☐	☐			
Filled out application forms.	☐	☐			
Proofread completed application forms .	☐	☐			
Applied for all financial aid and scholarships. (FAF, FFS, FAFSA)	☐	☐			
Essay written.	☐	☐			
Essay proofread.	☐	☐			
Received letters of recommendation.	☐	☐			
Submitted application packets to counselor.	☐	☐			
Requested transcripts to accompany applications.	☐	☐			
Made copies of applications and sent.	☐	☐			
Applied for post with French Foreign Legion just in case.	☐	☐			

Hey, What About. . . ?

More Stuff to Worry About

☐ Read it. . . _____

_____

_____

☐ Check It Out. . . _____

_____

_____

☐ Fill It Out. . . _____

_____

_____

☐ Think About It. . . _____

_____

_____

NOTES

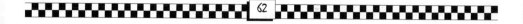

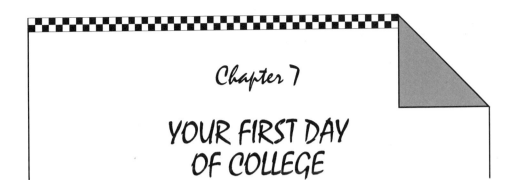

Chapter 7

YOUR FIRST DAY OF COLLEGE

When you do arrive at your new home away from home, your paradise found, your starting gate to higher education, your hunting ground for chicks and hunks, your springboard to fame and glory . . . your college, try to get yourself settled in right away. Unpack and set up your room in cooperation with your roommate. Make sure you are comfortable. Get all the little things such as extension cords, desk lights, bulletin boards, etc. that you forgot to buy beforehand. Set up your study area and unpack all your belongings so that you are comfortable and are not searching for calculators or black socks, while you are trying to make it to your first morning class of the year.

Go to all the orientation activities and explore the campus, if you have not done so already, so that you know where all your classes are located. Take a dry run through your daily class path. Make sure you know where to find the cafeterias, student activity offices, nurse's office, rest rooms, registrar's office, library, gym, local grocery store, drug store, bank and other relevant places.

Check out all the available clubs or student services that you might be interested in joining. See when their first meeting is and whose in charge. Remember to find out who your college counselor is and meet with them as soon as possible to map out your college course schedule.

My college counselor is_____

Room number_____Phone number_____

Ideally, arrive at your school as soon as they allow students to move in. Preferably, a day or two early to familiarize yourself somewhat with your new surroundings. This is a great opportunity to set up your room, check out part time jobs, get a checking account and take care of other nonacademic chores. When you do open your checking account make sure you have enough money in it to buy your books and any school or room supplies you might need. The first days on campus are hectic with thousands of other students trying to move in and get everything done just like you. Getting there as early as permitted might save you from waiting for elevators or maintenance personnel to fix a broken light socket, or find a better chair, etc. In addition you might be able to track down older students who have used books to sell. Also, ask them for any old tests or notes which were given with the courses. By getting all of these organizational tasks completed before school actually starts, you should be able to go into your first class relaxed and focused.

When registering, be sure to get there early and be sure it is your allotted time slot. Be certain you have every single piece of information required on your person before you get into line to register. Check before hand, by calling the Registrar's Office to find out exactly what is needed. Do not rely on anyone else to tell you what you need. Entire days can be wasted by standing in the wrong line or by not having all the registration information required. Before you head to college check into pre-registering and take advantage of this if allowed.

Begin your routine for general success and world dominance the very first day you arrive. If you have some course material, begin to read it. It is a good idea to wait until the first class of each subject before you go out and buy your notebooks etc. This way you will know exactly what kind of notebook, mechanical pencils or binders you will need. Do not forget to bring some type of notebook to all of your first classes so you can take any notes given. Chances are very good, in fact almost certain, you will receive homework your very first day. Welcome to college!!!

From day one, make time for exercising. Try out the college gym or swimming pool. Go hiking or play tennis. Find yourself a racquetball or jogging partner right away. Begin a good routine of eating right, sleeping right and exercising.

Your first week will be very busy with new classes, new faces and orientation activities, so you will need to immediately employ the scheduling and study habits you will read about later in this book. Make sure you write up and organize your weekly/monthly schedule right away following the scheduling tips given later in the book.

Also, believe it or not, some of you who have chosen to go away for school, might even get a little homesick. This is completely natural and is easily cured with time and by keeping yourself busy. **So let's get busy!**

Hey, What About. . . ?

More Stuff to Worry About

☐ Read it. . . _____

_____

_____

☐ Check It Out. . . _____

_____

_____

☐ Fill It Out. . . _____

_____

_____

☐ Think About It. . . _____

_____

_____

Chapter 8

WHAT DO I WANT TO STUDY AND DO WITH THE REST OF MY EXISTENCE?

A good starting place for choosing a major is to devote some thought to yourself. Think about what you would like to do each and everyday of your life. No, making a daily routine of guzzling gatorade and playing beach volleyball and then going to eat pizza and catching a movie would get really old after about 110 years. So try again; think about what you really would like to be doing:

- **on rainy gloomy days. . .**
- **on sunny beautiful days. . .**
- **when you are tired. . .**
- **when you are depressed. . .**
- **when you're feeling carefree and happy. . .**
- **with many people. . .**
- **with many other people you like. . .**
- **with many other people you do not like. . .**
- **with no other people. . .**
- **in the early morning. . .**
- **for free. . .**
- **in the evening. . .**
- **when all your friends are just kickin' back. . .**

If you have a particular interest, try to spend a day at work with someone in the profession. Go to work with your parents to see what they do. If they want you to be a doctor, then make them take you to work and show you why you should be in that profession. So what do you want to be when you grow up? Check one or fill in your room.

☐ Astrologist	☐ Navy Seal
☐ Archer	☐ Nirvana's Manager
☐ Accountant	☐ Nothing
☐ Barbeque Grill Tester	☐ Operator
☐ Bungee Jump Instructor	☐ Oceanographer
☐ Business Owner (What kind_____)	☐ Organ Player
☐ Cat Trainer	☐ Playboy
☐ Comedian	☐ Playgirl
☐ Cosmonaut	☐ Polo Pony Groomer
☐ Dishwasher	☐ Quasar TV Repair Person
☐ Dentist	☐ Quantum Leaper
☐ Daredevil	☐ Queen
☐ Editor Sports Illustrated	☐ Rodeo Rider
☐ Editor Sassy	☐ Revolutionary
☐ Editor Monster Trucks and Babes	☐ Restaurant Manager
☐ Fly Fisherman	☐ Safari Guide
☐ Fly Girl	☐ Sailor
☐ Fry Cook	☐ Sand Volleyball Player
☐ Gold Miner	☐ Teacher
☐ Gallery Owner	☐ Television Celebrity
☐ Ghost Researcher	☐ Trekky
☐ Historian	☐ Umpire
☐ Home Builder	☐ Undisputed Heavy Weight Champion
☐ Hood or Hoodess	☐ Underwear Model
☐ Inorganic Chemist	☐ Viva Las Vegas Video Producer
☐ Illustrator	☐ Violinist
☐ Inmate	☐ Veterinarian
☐ Judo Instructor	☐ Weatherperson
☐ Jet Pilot	☐ Waverunner Rental Person
☐ Jazz Musician	☐ Wildabeast Rancher
☐ King	☐ X-Ray Technician
☐ Kite Maker	☐ X-Student
☐ Kennel Owner	☐ Xylophone Designer
☐ Licensed something or other	☐ Yacht Captain
☐ Lighting Technician	☐ Yak Breeder
☐ Lamp Store Owner	☐ Yo MTV Raps Guest DJ
☐ Model Airplane Builder	☐ Zsa Zsa Gabor Fan Club President
☐ Mechanic	☐ Zombie
☐ Marshal	☐ Zoo Curator

I would like to be a _____ or _____

_____ or _____.

I think I would like to study _____in college.

Your college catalog or introduction packet will list all the available majors offered at a particular college. When choosing your major and the particular classes you will take, be sure to map out a 4 year course schedule, keeping in mind sports, activities or part time jobs. Your college advisor can assist you here, once you arrive on campus, however you should have a tentative schedule which you can discuss with your parents and high school counselor. Do not worry about changing majors once you are in college. This happens very often and usually the classes you are taking your freshman year are satisfying core requirements anyway. It's a good idea to take general classes your freshman year unless you are positive about what you want to go into. This provides a good balance and allows you to see what college is all about. Take at least one biology or health and nutrition course. Take one public speaking course and take at least one business and computer course. Usually, these can be conveniently worked into your core classes. Most colleges have a core program of liberal arts classes. You do not lose any time because all majors have some general courses which must be taken anyway.

Keep in mind, just because you major in Psychology, this does not mean you have to be a Psychologist. Business, marketing, criminal justice, political science, French, computer science or physics majors can go into any number of professions. Certain professions require certain majors. Medical school demands that your undergraduate curriculum emphasize biology and chemistry. You will need these classes in order to take the MCAT for admission into Medical School. Obviously, to be a dental hygienist you must major in Dental Hygiene. To be an elementary school teacher you  major in elementary education. Approach the selection of your major selection in light of your potential profession. Do not be too worried though, you can go in many different directions with most majors.

Be sure to review your potential major with your parents and counselor. They will be able to give you some hands on advice. In addition, make sure you speak to other students who are currently in your major and get the scoop on your classes and potential professors. (See chapter 14) Talking to some of the current students may also give you a potential

source for old tests and notes, a valuable college commodity. Just make sure the students you get notes from did well in the class.

When signing up for your classes, do not be too ambitious or unrealistic with yourself. During your first semester freshman year, sign up for only one class and make sure it is an easy one. This way you can spend most of your time partying and playing around. Sorry, that was a major typo. It should have read, "During your first semester freshman year, don't sign up for any classes. This way you will never skip any classes or get bad grades". Anyway, most colleges have credit requirements from 12-18 to qualify as a fulltime student, which is what you want to be if you plan on completing most major programs in four years. Also, most financial aid packages require fulltime status. However, you should stagger light classes with heavy ones so you do not overwork yourself. By talking to different students and by judging the subject matter and your own abilities, you will be able to determine what classes will be less demanding in terms of time and potential brain drain. Try not to

take more than two reading intensive courses or more than two courses which require lab time in any one semester. Also, don't sign up for three classes in a row on the same day. If possible, schedule so that you have two classes, then a break, then another one or two classes, etc.

Probably the greatest thing you could do to give yourself direction and spark your interest in a particular area of study, is to participate in an internship. I was a senior in college before I took an internship in the legal field. I became more excited about learning and education during this one semester internship than I had in my previous four years of college. I saw a purpose for some of my classes and received positive feedback about my own intellectual abilities, something the university grading scheme never seemed to provide. Some internships will give you college credits and some will pay you and give you credits.

Overseas semesters are the greatest! If you are interested in studying overseas, make sure your college has a program for it. This is highly recommended. Obviously, if you can plan this a year or two ahead of time, it will give you the opportunity to master the language.

Extracurricular activities: When in college you should participate in at least one extracurricular activity. Whether sports, drama, newspaper, band or student politics. They are ideal for scheduling discipline, resume building, and experience in general.

College sports are a "whole different ball game" than what you are used to in high school. Playing any collegiate sport from volleyball to football can take 3-4 hours out of each day. However there are a lot worse ways you could spend those hours. If you have the skills and can play a college sport, it is recommended you do. These 3-4 hours are spent staying in shape, getting disciplined, enhancing your abilities to work as a team and, hopefully, enjoying yourself. All in all, it's a great way to spend your time. If you do think you want to play a collegiate sport or have been offered a scholarship to do so, make sure you check out the facilities, practice routines, player benefits (tutors, special meal plans . . .) and coaches. Also, talk to a few of the current players and get their feedback on playing a sport in college.

Working: Chances are, most of you are going to have to work while in college. Be extremely careful in terms of scheduling your time. Before you register, carefully consider your time constraints with studying, work, travel, sports, socializing, family and friends. Develop a realistic schedule for yourself and do not take on too much.

Although it is wise to get a part-time job in some field related to your future profession, especially in your later college years, it is by no means essential. One of the best jobs a student can have while in college is as a waiter or waitress. You can work at night, you usually get a free 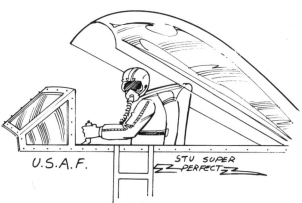 meal with each shift, you learn the importance of service and serving people, and you usually walk away with cash in your pocket. When looking for part time jobs, look for ones which have additional benefits, maybe working as a hotel front desk attendant on the evening shift. If things are slow, you can be reading or doing homework. Always check with your boss on this first and unless your boss is a sleazy, rotten, hostile, cruddy, loser, pig puke head butt face, then chances are he or she will not mind you devoting some time to your studies if it will not interfere with your work.

Oh yes, let us not forget grades, the all important yardstick indicator of success and destiny. This simply is not true! Grades, though, will open some doors for you, particularly, doors to higher centers of education like law and medical schools. In addition, some majors require you maintain a certain GPA in the courses in your field. Do not let grades get the best of you. Go to school to really learn about what you are interested in and the grades will fall in place. They will not do so magically, but if you are attentive to your classes, you should not have trouble. Grades fall when you let your discipline and interest decline.

There are certain classes which teach you what to do behind a desk or in a particular field, and then, there are classes which teach you about life. You want a few of these to balance out the business or chemistry courses. Some people might refer to these classes as slider classes, but try to take classes which challenge you spiritually. Life is much more then debits and credits or A's and F's.

One final note for students who someday plan to have a family of their own. You should look into majors that will lead to careers in which you can work fewer hours, control your own schedule and make good money. Sounds like what we all want anyway, right? Think about majors in the medical field or Teaching/Education which offer jobs where you will be able to work full time, part time and be able to schedule work around your family. Remember, with a family you are going to need day care so flexability and potential earnings should be considered.

Be supportive of your friends with whatever Majors or course of study they choose and hopefully they will be supportive of you. Do not get into the spineless habit of competing with your friends and classmates for grades etc.. **Compete with your books and win!!!!**

Hey, What About. . . ?

More Stuff to Worry About

☐ Read it. . . _____

_____

_____

☐ Check It Out. . . _____

_____

_____

☐ Fill It Out. . . _____

_____

_____

☐ Think About It. . . _____

_____

_____

Dorms, Sororities, Fraternities, Roommates

One of the greatest things about going to college is you will meet many new people. Some will no doubt become good friends and for many of you, one may even become your spouse. Yeah, can you believe it!!!

As a freshman going into college you will be assigned a roommate who has probably indicated some common traits with you on his or her housing application. Be sure to devote some thought to the application and answer honestly. Most colleges also allow you to choose your own roommate. If you and a friend are going to the same school and want to room together, this is usually not a problem. Let's not forget about compatibility though. If you think about it, chances are you have some friends who have remained your friends because you have never lived together. Just because you don't room with your high school buddy or buddess does not mean you won't be hanging out together. In fact, by both having different roommates you now have at least two more friends.

It is worthwhile to think about rooming with someone you do not know. It is a great opportunity to meet someone new and possibly any of their friends who are attending the same college. It is also good to get someone you don't know very well, as it helps you expand your horizons. The best choice of a roommate is definitely someone who studies and is neat. Having the same major can help and hurt. Good for questions on homework, usually maintain the same scheduling with tests, bad because you might be around each other too much. Remember dorm rooms are small and you have to get along.

My first roommate worked out nicely for me. He was from a different part of the country, a nonsmoker and was very studious. He would set a total of three alarms, not one, not two, but three. He called them back-up

vas in bed early and up early. Made almost no noise, except in
...ıg when he said I should be up anyway. He was obsessively neat,
.. ı missed the trash can with some paper he would put it on my bed and call
it negative reinforcement. Once we had a 20 minute wrestling match over a
new tube of toothpaste. He had taken it out of its box and wanted to start
using it by neatly rolling it up from the end, to assure maximum paste usage.
I wanted to punish this retentive behavior by squeezing the tube in the middle.
Well, the battle began, and I finally won, although it cost a broken light and
scattered books and papers. Anyway, a neat roommate is a good influence
and contributes to making your dorm room more inhabitable. If you want to
party and get crazy, fine, but you don't need to do it in your room.

It is important to set some rules to get along. Rules which govern the use of
your roommates or your stereo, tapes, cars, bikes, books, notes, pens, TVs,
clothes, perishables, as in supplies of "fermented beverages of choice," etc. In
my case, we had what we called "The Table of Conflict," a dresser which we
cleared off for an arm wrestling match to resolve disputes over items like
toothpaste, cleaning activities, the last beer, should the stereo be left on etc.. It
is paramount that you respect the possessions of others. Establish a borrowing
policy right up front. Always, always, always, always, always ask to borrow
something and return or repay whatever you borrow in a timely manner!!!!

When first moving in try not to move any of your clothes, etc. into the
dressers or closets, nor should you choose a bed or even a desk. Wait until
your roommate arrives and jointly decide who wants to use what dresser,
closet side, bed, etc. This is the best way to do it. Or even better, if you
can, talk prior to your first day and see who has what preferences. Maybe
your future roommate really wants to bring his or her stereo while you are
kind of "iffy". Maybe your future roommate already has a small refrigerator
so you won't need to buy or arrange to rent one. Maybe you prefer the top
bunk, maybe your roommate hangs all his or her clothes up, so they need a
lot of closet space but little dresser space. I hung nothing up so I needed no
closet space but I did need more dresser space. Many of these details can
be worked out over the phone. It is best to get these living condition items
mutually determined at the beginning of the year, or they could be an
ongoing headache later. Organize dorm room time schedules so one
person can have the room if they want. Work out study times when there
can be no TV or stereo on, and times when you might need some privacy.

Yes, when you room with someone you have never met then you do run
the risk of getting someone who resembles and acts like the creature from the

movie Alien, but if you do not like your roommate simply switch rooms. This might require a little bureaucratic juggling, or maybe just do it covertly. Do it though in an honest and friendly manner so you keep a friend and not create an enemy, unless of course they do resemble the *Alien*. Then blast'em and bolt!

Location of your dorm room is important. Try to request (firmly request) that you not be placed by the hall telephones, bathrooms, or entrance/exit doors. Just on our dorm floor alone we had 25 rooms with two or three people in each of them. The hall phones were always ringing. Although you don't have to always answer them, you hear all the rings and it usually takes 10 or 12 rings for someone to answer a hall phone. Certain floors are designated quiet floors. This is not a bad idea. In a few minutes you can be anywhere your friends are and still be able to get back and have a quiet place to study or sleep. Simply request to be placed in a "study dorm" or on a quiet floor. Rooming by the bathroom is also tough, a lot of BS and activity is centered around there so it is best to get away from it.

There are some basic tips about dorm life you should be aware of and prepare for accordingly. Dorms are not quiet places. If noise and commotion (there is a word you haven't heard for a while) bother you, definitely seek out a quiet floor or study dorm. Keep your doors locked when you are not there. This will prevent your things from being stolen, vandalized or worse yet, your room being targeted for a Panty Raid. So unless you do not mind your undies hanging from the flag pole or some other prominent spot, I suggest you keep your doors locked. Do not keep a lot of money or expensive jewelry in your room. If you must, at least hide it somewhere.

Probably the largest lifestyle decision you will make as you enter college is whether or not to join a fraternity or sorority. Not all colleges have a Greek system. Most large universities have a very large and active Greek organization. Most small colleges have either no Greek system or a very small one. It's a good idea to talk to friends who are in fraternities or sororities, and talk to friends who have chosen not to join them. Once you have decided whether or not to go Greek, then you have to decide which frat or sorority would be right for you. Keep in mind that you do not choose the frat or sorority, but they choose you.

Although there are differences across the nation with the Greek process, essentially they all work in about the same fashion. Fraternities and sororities have what are known as "rush parties", which are like open houses for potential "pledges" or new members. You would attend a few of these and see which house you would be interested in joining and which house is interested in you. It is during this series of rush parties, usually called "rush week" where they either "bid" you in or tell you to get lost. Once in, you become a pledge and, as a new member, would more than likely have to go through some preliminary orientation type activities as kind of an initiation. These vary from house to house and range from being informative tours of the house coupled with a history of the organization to just another party to welcome you aboard. Some Greek organizations, usually the sororities, require letters of recommendations from current members. This should be no big deal, you should have friends or friends who know friends before joining a house anyway. Serious hazing is supposed to be a thing of the past and is outlawed on most campuses. This does not mean you will not become a victim in some prank to welcome you into the house or to have you pledge your undying loyalty. Personally my loyalty stops when any other member of the human race wakes me up before I am ready. So, if you have a problem with being bothered for no reason, you might want to devote some thought to this.

☞ KEY ☞

1. Closet: **Do** divide space evenly. **Do** keep clean. **Do** put things you borrow from your roommate back where you found them. **Don't** let stuff pile up until a major fungi heapage forms. **Don't** borrow roommates stuff without asking. **Don't** let the semester go by without washing at least a few of the items in the closet.

2. Bathroom: **Do** rotate cleaning bathroom or sink area utilizing some form of disinfectant. (Coors light does not qualify as a disinfectant.) **Do** flush toilet after use. No da! (If you actually use that expression you probably do not use a toilet) **Do** be considerate of roommate in terms of time spent in the bathroom, hot water usage and general cleanliness. **Don't** use all of roommates toothpaste, shaving cream or shampoo without letting your roommate use all of your toothpaste, shaving cream and shampoo once in a while. **Don't** throw wet towels in corner of bathroom floor and let them sit for a week. **Don't** flush books, bad test papers (prior to review to see what mistakes you made) or broken blow dryers down toilets.

3. Phone: **Do** pay your share of the phone bill on time. **Do** schedule phone time with your roommate. **Don't** forget to get call waiting feature in case an emergency call comes in while discussing who did what to who at the party last night. **Don't** get into the habit of spending hours on the phone making long distance calls.

4. Communication: **Do** openly and honestly communicate with your roommate about any problems you might be having. **Do** give your roommate any and all phone messages that come in and have a spot to leave messages. (ie., answering machine good for phone messages). **Don't** hold in things that bother you

about your roommate or living conditions until you explode. Exploding is not good.

5. TV: **Do** schedule TV time with roommate. **Do** all of your homework first before you watch any TV. Never heard that before huh? **Don't** get in the habit of turning the TV on everytime you walk in the room. Heh try this, **Don't** bring a TV to college.

6. Stereo: **Do** get headsets so you can listen to tunes without bothering roommate. **Don't** listen to music while you study, unless its for Music Appreciation 204.

7. Refrigerator: **Do** get a small refrigerator to store healthy money saving munchies. **Do** replace whatever you take from your roommate. **Don't** drink your roommate's last beverage of choice.

8. Door: **Do** knock before entering rooms other than your own. **Don't** forget to lock your room when you leave.

9. Trash: **Do** empty your trash can once or twice a year. **Do** keep your room as clean as possible. **Don't** forget to recycle!!

10. Bed: **Do** be considerate of your roommate's sleep schedule. **Do** get an adequate amount of sleep. **Don't** sleep through morning classes.

11. Dressers: **Do** divide dresser space evenly. **Do** keep clothes and personal items neatly stored away. **Don't** leave expensive valuables out in the open or in an unlocked drawer.

12. Desk: **Do** set up a "Optima Study Place" for studying in your room. **Do** give you or your roommate's study time priority over TV, phone or stereo time. **Don't** forget to study.

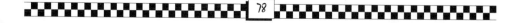

DO'S AND DON'TS OF THE DORM ROOM

(Also applies to Fraternity and Sorority Rooms)

Things to look for in a Fraternity and Sorority:

- House set up: Number of Rooms
- House GPA
- Calendar
- Prominent Alumni Members
- Current Members: Background
- Notorious for: (Partiers, Nerds, Jocks, Socialites, Granolas)
- House Rules on meals, study time, visitation
- Social Functions and rules governing them
- Proximity to and from campus

Advantages of joining a Fraternity or Sorority:

- Social opportunities. Continuous calendar of events and parties
- Good contacts network, both past and current members
- Files on courses, old tests, reference material
- Scholarships sometimes available
- Instant group of friends with common interests
- If you attended a smaller high school, fraternities and sororities
   can help a large university seem not so overwhelming

Disadvantages of joining a Fraternity or Sorority:

- Complete lack of privacy
- Lack of independence
- Additional dues and fees can add up
- B.S. initiation activities
- Risk of "Following the pack" and stereotyping
- Some houses require you to live in the Greek house until you are an
   active member. (Could be 2 years)

Obviously you still have tremendous social and networking opportunities if you do not join a frat or sorority, but they are definitely prevalent in the Greek system. All the same principles of dorm room survival apply to fraternities and sororities with a few pointers. Keep in mind most all your possessions (TV, stereo, clothes) can potentially become the possessions of all other house members, so communicate your wishes clearly if you have a problem with sharing. Kitchens are usually locked up after a certain time, so small refrigerators might be a good idea.

It is recommended to live on campus your first year and it is even mandatory at some colleges. It is definitely better in terms of meeting people and convenience. If you ever decide to move off campus then definitely live close to campus in a safe neighborhood. Even if you live off campus you can still get a meal plan. Chances are if you eat two meals a day this will be the most cost effective way.

Obviously, which ever lifestyle you choose you are always going to have to deal with people. Whether living in the dorm, a frat or sorority house, or off campus there are a few people you should make it a habit of getting to know. Your college catalog or introduction packet will probably contain this information. Make a list of these people and their phone numbers and keep it by the phone. At some point in your college career you will have to deal with the dean, academic dean, advisors, department heads, resident assistants and resident director. Their duties and powers vary from school to school, so make sure you know who handles what in case you need to speak to one of them.

You should make it a habit to be courteous to everyone. You never know when you might be 10 minutes late for dinner only to find the cafeteria doors closed and the meal ticket person closed down and not too anxious to let you in. Or your heater or air conditioner breaks in your dorm room and it's a billion below zero or a quadrillion degrees fahrenheit outside.

Besides the dorm, a Greek house or off campus, where else might a person live? Home sweet home, of course. It is definitely recommended that you not live at home, if possible, your freshman year in college. However if your financial situation dictates that you do, make sure you get involved in extracurricular activities so you don't miss out on the social life.

In conclusion, the people you meet in college can become college's most important contribution to you. Give everyone a fair chance, but do not get pulled down by whiners, wimps, negativos/negativas or bums. Hang out with exciting, up-beat, go getters, who encourage you to be your best and are always striving to be their best!

Hey, What About. . . ?

More Stuff to Worry About

☐ Read it. . . _____
_____
_____

☐ Check It Out. . . _____
_____
_____

☐ Fill It Out. . . _____
_____
_____

☐ Think About It. . . _____
_____
_____

Chapter 10
SURVIVAL TIPS

Meals, Health, Finance, Spiritual Breaks

There are 4 major maxims of general survival in college. Relentlessly follow these and let no man, woman, academic dean or animal stand in your way. Master these and you will become not only a graduate with a degree, but a graduate who is in great shape, has an ample cash horde, a clear head and isn't addicted to super beef burritos.

- **Do get in the habit of not always going out for fast food.**
  This zaps your energy level and pocket book.

- **Do get in the habit of exercising.**
  This increases your physical and mental endurance.

- **Do get in the habit of putting some money in savings every month.**
  This forms a lifelong habit of savings and gives you money for your Junior year spring break trip to Daytona.

- **Do get into the habit of taking a spiritual break.**
  This helps clear your head and helps you put things in perspective.

MEALS

1. Do get in the habit of not always going out for fast food.
This zaps your energy level and pocket book.

If there is one thing you need in college, it would be energy. An unhealthy fast food diet will soak up your energy. If you cannot control your urges for fast food fixes, try to develop a taste for the salad bars or other healthy menu items. Definitely avoid the fried foods. If you must eat fast food, eat heathy fast food. Most of your fast food chains have introduced some heathier options on their menu.

The average fast food order is around $4.00. If you go out for fast food on the average three times a week, that comes to 12 times a month or about 108 times during the school year. That comes to $432.00 just on fast food. Think about cutting your fast food binges to only one a week. This would save you almost $300.00 for the year. You can get pretty close to a week in Fort Lauderdale on Spring Break with that dough!

You will encounter no other culinary experience like you will during your college days, unless that is, you go into the Army or prison. University campuses vary from having decent cafeterias and restaurant-like snack bars to having a very mediocre cafeteria and some vending machines. For students attending a university with a cafeteria and meal plans, I strongly recommend taking full advantage of this service. The author of this book definitely recommends to sign up for a "three meal plan". This means you will have paid, as part of your tuition package, for three meals a day for the semester. This means everyday the cafeteria is

serving food you are entitled to have a breakfast, lunch and dinner. Sundays might be an exception with only two meals being served. If you are the kind of person who never gets up in the morning or never eats lunch, it is best to sign up for just a two meal plan.

For students watching their weight, beware, some university cafeterias offer many meals heavy in starch. If this is the case, take advantage of the salad bar. In addition, be sure to eat healthy foods. Most cafeterias have offerings which meet basic requirements. In addition, see if your college offers a course in nutrition. This would be a very valuable course and it might be able to be used to fill an elective regardless of your major.

Although college cafeterias are not known for their tasty cuisine, there are several major advantages which will be summed up this way, "They cook it for you, they clean up after you, and you get as much as you want".

For late night snacks, get a little refrigerator for your room. This will definitely save you money on fast food by allowing you to stock up on healthy munchies. A popcorn maker is excellent for late night, healthy, cost effective munchies.

For fraternities and sororities, their meal plans are an additional cost. One potential problem with Greek meals is, if your house is not conveniently located on campus then it might be hard to get back for lunch or dinner. Make sure you look into this before you sign up for your frat or sorority house meal plan versus a campus cafeteria plan.

2. Do get in the habit of physical exercising.
This increases your physical and mental endurance.

Obviously when an individual decides to enroll in a college or university they are signing up for a four year mental exercise program. Which is precisely the reason every student should, from the first day of classes until their last final, be involved in a regular pattern of physical activity as well. No matter what, find a physical hobby! Tennis, swimming, hiking, hang gliding, skiing, walking, running, crawling, dancing, weight lifting, aerobics, water volleyball, softball, baseball, horseback riding, golf, basketball, football or racquetball, whatever, and do it regularly.

Celeste and Kippy's Daily Activities

If you are playing a college sport, great. If not, find a hobby or sign up for an intramural sport which forces you to stay in shape while you are really doing something you enjoy.

If you do not know how to play any sports, sign up for a (PE) Physicall Education class like Aerobics or Racquetball, you'll get a few extra credits while staying in shape and possibly start a lifelong hobby.

In order for your mind to work to its fullest potential, your body must be in shape. Staying physically fit allows you to pay better attention in class, learn and retain information faster (which means less time studying) and gives you the energy to accomplish more each day. This fact is easily seen when you go two weeks without any physical activity. You will feel your energy level and enthusiasm drop off. Try to get out and exercise just once and see how much better you feel. Make this a regular part of each day, even if it's only for 1/2 hour.

Besides staying in shape, it is important to have a physical and dental check up at least once a year. When you get to college, if it is out of your hometown, immediately find a local doctor and dentist in conjunction with the school's medical staff. Dental check ups are a breeze. All you do is meet a dental hygienist who, as part of their training, need to practice their lessons by working on volunteer students/patients. You could easily get your teeth thoroughly cleaned twice a year for $5 or even free. So you end up helping a friend, plus taking care of yourself. They can provide you with a basic check up and advise you if a dentist is necessary. When it comes time for them to practice giving injections, introduce them to another friend of yours.

Physicals are a good idea also. A physical exam prior to embarking on your new life of daily exercise is essential. Have this done before you leave for college. An annual physical and a complete blood test to check cholesterol levels, etc. is advisable, even when you are in college. In addition, an HIV test might also be a good idea, and remember if you are not going to abstain from sex until you are married, which by the way, is the ultimate way to avoid disease, unwanted pregnancies and at least a few emotional upsets, then remember to practice the safest sex possible every time!

I know you have heard it two billion times, so here is two billion and one, if you eat right and exercise regularly through your college years, you are establishing one of the most important habits of your life.

3. **Do get in the habit of budgeting and putting some money in savings every month.**
   This forms a lifelong habit of savings and gives you money for your Junior year spring break trip to Daytona.

Even if you do not have any money, you should begin a habit of making a deposit into a savings account every month. Even if it consists of only change you find on the floor or in the coin return of vending machines. Whenever you get paid, get your allowance, win a card game or find money, always take a portion and immediately deposit it into a savings account. When you have accumulated enough you can transfer it to a more sophisticated savings instrument like a money market account or a mutual fund. If you have one of those already started then add to it every month or, if there is a minimum, you should be able to acquire that amount every two months. Preferably, see if your parents will set up a matching program with you. They have to match any amount you deposit. They will probably want to maintain the account in both names, so you don't run off to Europe unannounced with your millions. If you are working, check out and see if your employer has sponsored savings plans or if they will automatically deduct a certain amount from your check and put it into your savings.

By only saving $35 dollars a month or $8.75 a week for 9 months and not eating fast food more than once a week (as opposed to 3x a week) for 9 months, you will have saved approximately $767.00. How's that for a nice trip to celebrate getting through a year of college. And if you talk your parents into a matching program, you've got $1,534.00 not including interest. And if you continue this program until you've graduated four years later including the summer months, then you will have $7,968.00 for a nice graduation gift to yourself. Sure you will have outstanding loans for college to pay back, but you will pay those back from the money you earn from the job you get with your college degree. Even if your parents do not participate by matching, you still could have almost $4,000.00 in the bank at graduation time. Sounds too good to be true? Just try it and see. Put it

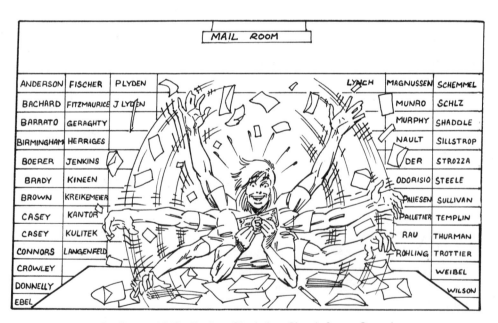

Traditional Life Saving Birthday Check from Grandma

away every month and forget about it, it no longer exists. Only $8.75 a week and no more than one fast food frenzy a week.

It is a good idea to get yourself a credit card when you go to college. This way you can eat out like mad and immediately buy a new stereo and then tap your card out so you won't have any money for an emergency. Once again, wrong! Credit cards are a good tool for emergencies or trips. They also help you discipline yourself by having to pay them off regularly. Talk to your parents about helping you get a card. Also set up a checking account and make sure you balance it regularly. Some banks will set up an overdraft protection program which is not bad idea in case you accidentally write a check when there is not enough money in the account. Bad check fees can add up fast and look rotten on a credit report.

It definitely pays to have your financial situation under control and budgeted. You do not need two worries, studies and bills.

Spiritual

4. **Do get into the habit of taking a spiritual break and relaxing.**
   This helps clear your head and helps put things in perspective.

I used to take my dogs for walks in the mountains to relax. Whether it be that or going to a house of worship, listening to music, working as a volunteer one day a month, always take some time to clear your head. Remember, as part of physical exercise, complete relaxation is good also, whether it be a total vegetation session with your headphones on and "Nirvana" playing or a walk in the park with your dog.

Here are a few other survival tips:

It is highly recommended that you talk to someone who is attending your college choice and living in the same place you plan on living (dorm or house, etc.) and ask them what to bring. If you have not been away from your little home front for any major durations then, while packing, you should think about an average day and week in your life and determine what things your wear, use and need. This should help you pack. Don't worry you can always call home collect and have stuff shipped UPS.

Remember, there are definitely a few things you do not want to forget to stick in your college survival kit. They are:

1. Calculator
2. Dictionary
3. Thesaurus
4. Computer (optional, school will have them)
5. Calling card (for emergencies only)
6. Credit Card (for emergencies only)
7. Desk Calendar (schools sometimes provide these)
8. Assignment Note Book
9. Laundry Instructions and fold up hamper. Remember to watch your stuff, study while laundry is being done.
10. Bike and lock.
11. Small Refrigerator. Economize on eating out and snacks.
12. Desk light.
13. Insurance- so you do not have to worry about anything getting stolen.
14. Address Book
15. Pictures from Home

Add your own:

16. _____	25. _____	34. _____
17. _____	26. _____	35. _____
18. _____	27. _____	36. _____
19. _____	28. _____	37. _____
20. _____	29. _____	38. _____
21. _____	30. _____	39. _____
22. _____	31. _____	40. _____
23. _____	32. _____	41. _____
24. _____	33. _____	42. _____

Remember, even though college is a place to experience new things, being a victim of a crime is not one which is recommended. Don't walk around alone at night or try to find your way around a strange part of any city, not even once. Hang out in groups whenever possible and get the scoops from older students on what areas are potential trouble spots.

Hey, What About. . . ?

More Stuff to Worry About

☐ Read it. . . _____
_____
_____

☐ Check It Out. . . _____
_____
_____

☐ Fill It Out. . . _____
_____
_____

☐ Think About It. . . _____
_____
_____

Chapter 11

ATTITUDE

The attitude one has during his or her college career can be the single most important indicator of success or failure. Since this is such an important topic, I have devoted an entire chapter to the subject. Before you read this chapter, I am going to ask you to clear your mind of all distracting thoughts such as upcoming tests, parents, boyfriends, girlfriends, parties, no parties, big games, little games, big sisters, little brothers, homework, MTV, VH1, teachers, so on & so on . . . Just sit back, close your eyes and relax for about 2 minutes then after you feel your mind is empty, you know, the feeling you get right before an Algebra test, open your eyes and begin to read.

It would be a nice world if everyday of your life you could:

- Party
- Travel to Europe with your boyfriend or girlfriend
- Eat pizza and drink Dr. Pepper for breakfast, lunch and dinner
- Suntan on a Bahamian island in a hammock
- Party
- Watch MTV (You already do that, so what's the big deal?)
- Ride a motorcycle across the USA
- Go shopping at the mall with Luke Perry
- Have En Vogue be your date for the senior prom
- Find a million dollars
- Party

Add your own:

- _____
- _____
- _____
- _____

However, the real world, which, by the way, is the one you live in or at least are supposed to be living in, is usually less than ideal. In college you are going to find yourself having to do many things you might not exactly love doing. Scheduling, late night studying, missing parties, not eating out, taking tests, working part time jobs, writing papers, troubled or no relationships, getting sick and possibly more severe personal or family crisis.

What are some of the things that can, and will happen to erode your positive sun shiny attitude? Here are a few of the more common. Please rate them and add any of your own.

___ Bad test scores

___ Illness

___ Guilty feelings from skipping class

___ Roommate troubles

___ Trouble with your teachers or coaches

___ You're behind in your reading

___ Being too skinny

___ Being too fat

___ Being homesick

___ Nasty letters from your boyfriend or girlfriend back home

___ No letters from your boyfriend or girlfriend back home

___ Really bad test scores

___ Having to study or work when you want to party

___ Not getting along with friends

___ A personal family crisis

___ Not liking yourself

___ Lousy weather

___ Other_____

___ Other_____

___ Other_____

___ Other_____

___ Other_____

___ Other_____

It seems when one thing goes wrong, everything goes wrong. Do not let bad situations snowball. It is important that you act right away upon any situation that is causing a bad attitude. Anything that is affecting you is causing anxiety, either negative anxiety like a bad test score or a fight with a friend, or positive anxiety, like a good test score or waiting for a sporting event to start. Anxiety is like energy, it excites you and affects you both mentally and physically. The best way to counter negative energy is to turn it into productive positive energy.

A foolproof solution to problems that get you down, taken from world renown author/expert psychologist, Dr. Karl Menninger's criteria for emotional maturity is to "sublimate anxiety into productive outlets". What this means is when you receive a 54% on a calculus test, you should immediately run over your calculus teacher repeatedly with a big truck. Sorry, I do not think it is a good idea, especially since your calculus teacher has been devoting him or herself for the past few weeks to teaching you how to pass calculus tests. So then you should repeatedly run yourself over with a big truck. Buzz, wrong again, there is no college class anywhere worth that much. So what should you do?

What I believe Dr. Menninger is saying is, first, you should sit down and say:

Normal human reaction:
> "This really bites the big one that I got so totally reamed on that stupid test!!! "

Scientifically credentialed reaction:
> "I am experiencing post test depression resulting from the poor academic marking I scored."

Then you should ask yourself;

Normal human reaction:
> "Why did I get so completely blown away on that test? I must be stupid! Do I study more? Did I study the wrong things? I should have asked that question in class. I think I better drop out and move to the Himalayas and become a Yak breeder!!!"

Scientifically credentialed reaction:
> "I believe some contemplation on my poor performance could help me to reexamine my past study patterns and by engaging in open discussions with my professor I can clarify test topics where I faltered and refocus my studies and patterns."

Then you should;

Normal human reaction:
> "Yes, is this Speedy Travel? Yes, Miss Travel Agent, a one way ticket to the Himalayas please."

Scientifically credentialed reaction:

> "I believe it best that I immediately recompose myself and head to the library to get a head start on the next Calculus exam. I will use all of this hostile energy inside me and direct it at mastering this material, page by page, paragraph by paragraph, problem by problem, therefore enabling me to pass calculus, get my degree, get the job I want and then be able to travel to the Himalayas on my own terms and not have to survive by picking up Yak manure for a living.

If you do not believe what we just discussed, then try it for yourself. Next time something hits you and is causing a bad attitude and depression, no matter how small, immediately work on something you have to get done. If you get a bad test score, then immediately go study for just one hour and see how much better your attitude becomes. Or, if you just had a fight with a friend, go to an aerobic step class. Whenever confronted with something that "bums you out", is a "mental downer" or "merely

Steve and Kelmar trading places. . .

depresses you to the max" then simply begin to do just one little productive thing, whether it is 100 sit-ups or organizing your history notes. Your initial cause for depression or anxiety will probably still be there, but you will already feel better about dealing with it since you have taken control and are doing something productive.

This technique can be applied and should be applied for one of the major causes of depression or bad attitudes, that is, not liking who you are. You know what I mean, the one thing you always wanted to change about yourself, but it just seems impossible! You begin to work toward it, maybe it's a first jog to lose weight, or it's the first week of a new semester and you are not going to fall behind, and sure enough, after maybe two workouts or three days of good studying, you blow it off. Then you find yourself feeling like a worthless loser, drowning in a sea of self pity, being pulled down by the weight of a major bad attitude or MBA. But you know what? You are a worthless loser, so go ahead and drown. But you say, "I am not a loser, but I say you are, but you say your not, you are, are not, are to, are not, are to" . . .and then the theme from Rocky starts to play "Na na na na na na na na na na na Na Na Na Na Na Na Na Na Na Na Na Na Na Na Na Na.....Gonna fly now, won't be long now, na na na . . .Na NAAAAA!!! And then you start to take that first step. You go to the aerobics class or you read the one chapter ahead of time. See how great you feel after just that first step. Try to sustain this for only one day and see how great you feel after just one day where you studied and exercised and packed a tremendous amount of productive activities into one day. Then try to sustain this for just one week! Soon you will be unstoppable achieving absolutely everything you set out to accomplish!!

Compare this to the MBA acquired by not working toward your goal. There is no comparison! Don't worry if you stop after only three or four work outs or two chapters. You simply start again and this time maybe you'll make it a little longer. You might even stay up on all of the assignments and chapters through a whole set of material for a particular test. And then, maybe, you'll get a decent grade on your test and find yourself with all sorts of energy and it is really a lot easier than blowing things off and playing catch-up.

So, go ahead, get depressed, bummed and or really down, and try this sure fire "poor attitude buster" technique. Remember begin with just one little productive action and see how your attitude starts to turn around. Begin practicing this technique now and by the time college rolls around you'll be undepressable.

Hey, What About. . . ?

More Stuff to Worry About

☐ Read it. . . _____
_____
_____

☐ Check It Out. . . _____
_____
_____

☐ Fill It Out. . . _____
_____
_____

☐ Think About It. . . _____
_____
_____

Chapter 12

PROCRASTINATION:
THE COLLEGE STUDENT'S #1 ENEMY

Procrastination:

(Taken from *Roget's College Thesaurus in Dictionary Form*, A Signet Book and enhanced by yours truly.)

n. postponement, delay, dilatoriness; negligence, omission.
v. let slip, lay aside, overlook, disregard, pass over, blow off, latered, nixed

see neglect:
carelessness, heedlessness, thoughtlessness, dereliction, looseness, absence of mind.

Procrastinator:

neglector, trifler, waster, wastrel, blow off artist, drifter, slacker, time burning bum, worthless derelict, lazy butt head.

I am just not into writing this now, I think I'll check it out later.

Chapter 13
Scheduling Habits: QST & QLT

Assuming you go away to school, your first day of college will be the first day of a new level of independence you are probably not accustomed to. No, "Have you done your homework yet?", No "Be home by 11:30!". No "Babysit your younger brother until we come home!". No "Why haven't you brought a book home from school in the last 6 weeks?". No. "No's!!". College is probably the first time no one, who by their genetic right of paternal dominance and their legal rights as owner of the house in which you live, is telling you what to do and when to do it. While this new lifestyle of independence, void of any immediate parental or guardian control, is totally exhilarating and, when first encountered, makes you feel like launching yourself into a four year party frenzy, it also is somewhat scary. Never before in your life have you been handed such an opportunity, whereby you can make use of your time in almost anyway you want. You can sleep in everyday until 2:00pm. You can eat pizza for breakfast, lunch, dinner and dessert. You can leave your bed unmade, or not even sleep in a bed. You can watch MTV at 1:00pm in the afternoon and 1:00am in the morning. Each hour, of each day, except on your visits back to your parent's home, is yours to spend however you want. Sure you are going to have classes to go to, and you are human, (if we stretch the definition for some of you) so you will need to eat once in awhile. Everyone hopes you continue to shower and practice basic hygiene. In addition, you will have various activities such as jobs, sports and the all important leisure activities to partake in. However, as a rule, you will be on your own to choose how to spend each minute of each day. And let me tell you, this power is greater than the "force" itself, so use it wisely!!!!

You can choose to let each day idle away, accomplishing only minimal tasks or you can attack each minute, each hour or each day like it is your last day on the planet. Let's think about something: There are 365 days in a year, 24 hours in a day and 60 minutes in an hour. If you sit on your butt for only 10 minutes a day, at the end of a year you will have used up

More of Steve and Kelmar. . .

approximately one week of your year or should I say rear (allowing for sleep of course). If you blow off 20 minutes a day you would have spent 2 weeks of your year doing nothing. Let's think of it another way. Lets say you spend just 1 hour everyday doing something, anything. It could be extracurricular reading, exercise, painting, volunteer work, whatever. At the end of one year you would have spent approximately an entire month devoted to whatever you wanted. If you can schedule yourself properly and use your time wisely, you can actually get an extra month a year, every year. That means if you can use just one hour a day in a useful fashion (as opposed to punching the remote control) between the ages of 18 and 70, you will have spent approximately 4.3 years devoted to whatever you choose. Think about what sitting on your butt doing nothing for four years does to a person's mind, not to mention his or her other end.

Do not fool yourself here! Do not schedule all 8:00am classes for everyday of the week, convincing yourself this will force you to get up early and make the most out of the mornings, unless you know you will get up. Take a serious look at yourself here, if you are a morning person then schedule accordingly. Will you get up in time? Will you pay attention? Or are you a Voyeuristic Collegiate Vampire (VCV), who prefers to hang out with the other vampires roaming the dark quiet corridors of the college at night searching for books to suck the knowledge out of, which is fine too? Just remember to crash sometime before the sun comes up.

Now let's take a minute to discuss two very important aspects of scheduling and time. They are QUALITY LEISURE TIME (QLT) and QUALITY STUDY TIME (QST);

Quality Leisure Time ("QLT") is being able to kick back and do whatever you want without having to worry about what you aren't doing or should be doing (homework,etc.). Otherwise kicking back doing what you want to, without having to worry about what you are putting off to take this time. It is 10 times more refreshing and rejuvenating then nonQLT.

Classic example: All your friends want to go out to the bowling alley or the _____ (fill in favorite hang'en spot) on a Wednesday night at 7:00pm. You have a homework set due on Friday. You know you should be, in fact you need to, spend sometime tonight getting most of your problems done because they are not easy and you do not want to have to cram it all in tomorrow night because you have a full day tomorrow. So what do you do:

A. Blow off your assignment and sprint to the _____ beating your friends there and already submerged in party activities by the time they arrive.

B. Blow off your assignment and go to the _____ with your friends and possibly have a lousy time because you know tomorrow will be a drag with all the work you have to do.

C. Bring your homework to the _____ and try and do a problem between each bowl, each piece of pizza or whatever.

D. Tell your friends you will meet them later and study for an extra two hours, getting your homework nearly finished and still making it to the _____ by the time the action starts exuberant with a major QLT rush!

If you picked A, you are absolutely normal, but weak! If you picked C, you're confused and live in a fantasy world and will bowl the worst game of your life! And if you picked D, then you are correct and have maximized party attendance by utilizing the secrets of QLT .

Simply say to yourself "I am going to study until 9:00pm" or give yourself a number of problems to complete before you go out. Then, when you do go out, you will feel much more relaxed and will not worry about the homework you are blowing off. Works well on Friday night, all study areas are quiet, if you can just study until 9 or 10pm then you can still go out and usually things are just rolling by then.

Quality Study Time ("**QST**") is being able to study utilizing the maximum amount of focused concentration because you have partied or enjoyed your QLT and are anxious to learn and accomplish something academically productive, which like relaxing, is also a natural human desire. With QST you can achieve much greater learning in much less time.

And while you are scheduling, make sure you schedule some "**TVT**" (=total vegetation time). This is closely associated with QLT.

In college, you will notice teachers and students become jerks around midterms. Scheduling will keep you from becoming a jerk. Yeah, and you thought there was nothing you could do to stop from becoming a jerk. Everybody will be jockeying for missed notes, reference books and copying machines. The library and study areas will be busier than usual. If you have scheduled yourself you will not be scrambling to catch up and will remain extremely cool during this otherwise frantic time.

Remember when you increase your study time dedicated to one subject, the world does not stop. You have other classes and homework which you have to stay up on. Proper scheduling is the best way to handle all of your teachers who give you work regardless of your other class loads. Things seem to always come up at the same time. It is important to stay on top of things so around midterms or before breaks you can take on any additional loads given to you by teachers who are cramming to get in all the material they promised at the beginning of the term.

Whatever you do, get a large desk calendar and a pocket calendar/assignment book. At the beginning of each semester note your long term projects such as papers and tests. Write "ticklers" to remind you when to start reviewing or when to have first draft done by, or 2nd book read by, etc. Always give yourself early deadlines so you stay ahead of the game. Give yourself time to work through material you do not understand and be prepared even if some crisis pops up a week before your test. (See chapter 16 on studying)

Try to establish a pattern for each of your days. Right after your first set of classes of any semester, sit down and write up your daily and monthly calendar. It should contain blocks of time for classes, studying, eating and exercising. Keep in mind every hour you spend in class requires an hour or more outside the classroom. When writing up your schedule first fill in your classes, then your study blocks outside regular class time(1 hour class = 2 hours outside studying), then your sleep, meals, and exersize time. After those items have been logged, you will know how much time you have for extracurricular activities, work and partying.

When you are setting up your schedule, try to get most of your work done early in the day. This is the time you have the most energy and enthusiasm for getting homework done. There is a greater tendency to blow things off at night. In addition this leaves nights more open for part-time jobs or social engagements. If you play a sport or simply prefer to study late at night, that is fine. It really depends on the individual here.

What's more important than "night vs. day" is "studying vs. not studying". If you like to study at night, then by all means set up your schedule to study at night. Hopefully, it's not because you put off studying until night time, but because you find yourself ready or able to study at this time.

You would be surprised how much productive time a person can squeeze into one day. And this is not just academically productive time, but also party time! Let's do a "How Much Time Do I Waste" Analysis on ourselves to see how much more productive time we could be utilizing. Once you are in college do an occasional **TWA or Time Waste Analysis** to see if you have fallen into any wasteful patterns. Simply use this format.

Fill in daily activities:

	Mon.	Tue.	Wed.	Thu.	Fri.	Sat.	Sun.
7:00am - 8:00am							
8:00 - 9:00							
9:00 - 10:00							
10:00 - 11:00							
11:00 - 12:00							
12:00 - 1:00pm							
1:00 - 2:00							
2:00 - 3:00							
3:00 - 4:00							
4:00 - 5:00							
5:00 - 6:00							
6:00 - 7:00							
7:00 - 8:00							
8:00 - 9:00							
9:00 - 10:00							
10:00 - 11:00							
Time saved after removing useless activities							
Hours							

and give yourself an occasional check up. Take this chart with you, for one week, and fill in exactly what you did during the time slots indicated. Fill in everything from taking a shower and getting dressed to working your job, sports practice and talking on the phone. When it is completed do a "time wasted" check of each hour and activity.

After a week of logging your activities, see where you could save time. Add up the time you save by removing or limiting activities which are not really necessary, such as watching too much TV, talking on the phone constantly or an excessive amount of playing Nintendo. Check to see how much time you could be devoting to productive activities, such as reading or exercising. Have someone else, say your parents, (yeah that's an idea,) review your chart and see which activities they would cut out. You will probably find you are able to squeeze an hour more a day out of each day, just by cutting out some of the useless activity. Which calculates to an extra seven hours a week. Yeah, I know, you're gonna be the World Champion Nintendo player and make millions going to tournaments. Just in case you don't make it to the Nintendo finals, give yourself an honest evaluation. Don't go overboard, remember you need QLT and TVT also, and they are as valuable as work or homework time.

Go ahead and see how easy college will be when you schedule versus cram. All nighters, rush papers overdue problem sets will drive you nuts. Scheduling will allow you to do more each day while minimizing stress. Once you handle a mere three weeks of school with tests, homework and papers, utilizing proper scheduling, you will never want to go back to cramming.

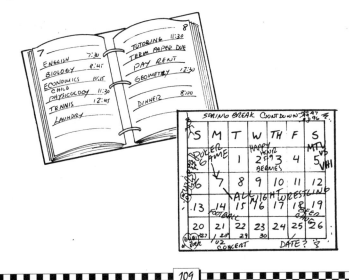

Hey, What About. . . ?

More Stuff to Worry About

☐ Read it. . . _____

_____

_____

☐ Check It Out. . . _____

_____

_____

☐ Fill It Out. . . _____

_____

_____

☐ Think About It. . . _____

_____

_____

Chapter 14
THE CLASS

Classes and classrooms are the format and the forum by which most, if not all academic institutions conform their teaching agendas. You are no stranger to classes or classrooms. You have been attending them since kindergarten. I wish all levels of academic study were centered around graham cracker snacks, recess, and those little woven mats you used to take naps on, but unfortunately they are not.

The concept of the classroom actually developed thousands of years ago. Cavemen and cavewomen of the Neanderthal era would collect around their fires in their caves and one of the elder cavepersons who knew the ways of survival would teach the young cave dwellers Hunting 101, Introduction to FireBuilding, Intermediate Dinosaur Fleeing and History of the World (which by the way was a slider course at the time because there just wasn't much history to remember). If any of the young cavepersons would skip a lesson, they would receive demerits and get sent to the principal's cave and have to stay after and carve rocks, unless they got their cave girlfriend or cave boyfriend to forge an absentee slate (slip) which would get them back into the lessons without any trouble.

These learning sessions, known as classes, vary from a 45 minute engrossing discussion on interesting and relevant topics to, 3 hour torture lectures which leave you asleep and confused, as if that thought isn't confusing enough. In this chapter, we are going to teach you to be one with the class, one with the classroom. You will learn to savor each class, to absorb all which is recited to you, and to yes, even understand it. The four walls, which for some of you have grown to symbolize imprisonment, torture, boredom and something to avoid, will now become your best friend, you will be begging for more class time, you will want to start sleeping in these classrooms, and I don't mean during class.

College classrooms come in all shapes and sizes from small 20 seat four walls and a chalkboard to mega 300 seat auditoriums with electric boards, overhead projectors and computer generated slide presentators. No matter what size, or dimensions, the classroom is, you must immediately begin to think of it in different terms. Not the traditional "I gotta be here for a hour and listen to this stuff" place. Think of the classroom for what it is, a room, or a place where there is someone who's job it is to help you improve yourself. A workout room for your brain. Every time you enter one of these rooms realize and plan on helping yourself become a better more intelligent person. This is great, college is going to give me four years, 18 hours a week of workout sessions to improve "me". They are going to supply dozens of different personal mental fitness instructors whose only goal in life is to help me learn.

You must think of each classroom and each class as your own. You are paying for them so get as much as possible out of each of them. Go into each class and tear as much information out of your professors as possible. There will come a day, and it will be sooner than you think, when you will realize it is not cool to be stupid. Walking around with your shoes untied, skipping classes and not studying is cool for about a minute.

When you are actually in a classroom there are a few pointers on classroom etiquette which will help you pay attention and get the most out of class.

Pointer #1   Place Yourself:

Seating is a critical element of the classroom. Studies have been done on the relation to student seat location and academic performance along with teacher perception. Basically, if you want to perform well and get good grades in a class you should sit in the front row or toward the front in the middle. This position almost forces you to pay attention and limits the possibility of your falling asleep. The back and the sides are harder to pay attention with greater chances of talking to other students or becoming distracted. Some people like the middle where they feel safe and think they can blend in and avoid being victimized by merciless questioning for which some professors are notorious. Others, like myself prefer the sides, where you do not feel trapped. Sit where you feel the most comfortable. Vary where you sit from class to class. It can provide you with a little variety and keep some classrooms from becoming major boreboxes. The most important thing is to sit somewhere in the classroom during class.

Pointer #2   Pay attention:

What is the hardest thing to do in the world, Getting a date with Jason Priestly or Mariah Carey? Getting tickets to a U2 concert? or Paying Attention during your classes? As you already know it is not easy to pay attention through 50 minute or an hour and a half long class. Especially if it's a continuous lecture on _____(fill in something that bores you until you puke).

To help you pay attention, the first thing you need to do is make sure you are taking care of yourself physically. Yes, get plenty of sleep and exercise. If possible schedule some exercise before classes which are particularly straining on your mind. Even a nice walk outside before the class will help clear your head.

Secondly, stay focused on the material. This is difficult especially if you are already in the habit of day dreaming during class. You must break this habit by forcing yourself to stay focused on the material for the entire class period and you must break this habit now, today!!! It is a constant battle, especially with classes you are not so hip on. At first you will find yourself going in and out of focus several times during any one class, but after several classes where you really try hard to pay attention and successfully do so for the whole duration of the class, the discipline will get easier. So begin with the very next class! Force yourself to stay focused the whole time right until the last minute. And during the next class, do the same, stay focused the whole class period. Work hard at this until you have it down. A few items which will make it easier for you to pay attention are wear comfortable clothes, utilize #1 above and place yourself properly in addition to utilizing #3 and #4. Also keep your eyes forward, not on the clock, but on the teacher or between the teacher and your notes. Also sit straight up in your chair, do not slouch or rest on your elbow.

In addition, I am not sure what you are used to in high school, but the days of talking in class are over. 99% of college professors do not consider this an issue and you will become a nonissue in class if you decide to carry on conversations during class. There are quite a few students in the class who are paying their own tuition and don't like to miss lecture material due to worthless ramblings about what you could have done the night before but something happened right before you were gonna do it.

Pointer #3   Participate:

Most students are not big participators. Some are simply shy, others don't know the answers and some don't want to be defined by their peers (note: not real friends) as butt kissers. If you have a question then ask it. The reason you are in the classroom is to learn. The reason the teacher is there, is to teach. Make them earn their money. Do not let them race through a lecture without explaining clearly anything that you do not understand. The easiest way to prevent covering something in a class you do not understand is to put your stupid hand in the air and get the answer before you let the teacher move on. Do not let yourself fall behind in a lecture. The second you are lost, ask a question. Do not be afraid to ask any questions a class lecture might prompt you to think of, even if it is not exactly on the subject, after all the reason you are in college is to learn and expand your mind.

The other major form of class participation is taking notes. Acquiring good note taking skills is essential! If you have doubts about your note taking techniques, simply take a minute or two after each of your classes. Show each of your professors your notes for their class and ask each of them their opinion. This should give you a variety of useful hints on how to improve your note taking skills. You can make this a life-long habit, although it will not be necessary after awhile. Whenever you begin a new class, ask the teacher for 5 or 10 minutes and have him or her review your notes on the lecture. Doing this just once will give you some useful direction and feedback on your notes. Also, try to get to each class a minute early so you can get your notes ready and be prepared to listen as soon as the class begins.

A few simple pointers on note taking are:

1. Write down the main points of discussion and leave plenty of room between them to fill in more detailed information.

2. Do not worry about getting everything, the main points will allow you to reference your text book and fill in the blanks. However do not be afraid to ask the teacher to slow down if he or she is going to fast.

3. As soon after class as possible, recopy and reorganize your notes. Taping lectures and writing notes are also good ideas. A good rule

of thumb, no, let's make that a great rule of thumb, is to take notes during class and recopy and organize them as soon as possible after class. If the lectures are too intense to keep up with note taking. Relax and listen to the lecture while taping it. Then, later, copy and organize you notes from your tape. Some people are not an advocate of this approach. Decide for yourself what helps you learn. Ask professors for permission before you tape their lectures.

Pointer #4   Perception:

One of the biggest problems I had with school was the perception that a lot of the material I was learning would never be necessary in the real world. Well, you know what, college is the real world. If you do well in college, then you can go on with your education and into any profession you desire. College is not only training you for your future job, but it is an exercise for your mind and discipline, so you will be able to handle anything in life. Do not expect to immediately see applications for what you are learning, but do look for ways a particular subject will help you, even if one is not evident. A business problem in accounting, for instance; put yourself in one of the person's shoes in the problem, and act as though it is your money. This should grab your attention. Or, relate it to a real life experience you have had or are having. Ask, or even force the teacher to give you real life applications for problems or items they lecture on. They will love you for this.

Pointer #5   Prepare:

Go to classes prepared. Keep up on your reading and read chapters before you hear the teachers lecture on them. Do your homework. If you do not understand something then go on to the next problem and ask your professor at the next class. Reread your notes and make sure you understand the material you have covered to date. If you go to every class prepared you will never have to be worried about getting called on and not knowing the answer. If by some remote chance, once or twice in your college career, you are called on and do not know the answer, simply look the teacher straight in the eye and fake a huge combination heart, allergy, brain trauma attack and race out of the room knocking over desks and hitting walls. Be careful though, this will work only once, maybe twice per teacher per year. Actually, if you do not know the answer, simply tell the teacher, "As a matter of fact, I was just about to ask you that very same question". The teacher will then have to answer it and you are off the hook.

In order for the above five pointers to be effectively utilized, you must make sure you are in the classroom. You certainly do not want to miss the first class of a semester when the "syllabus" (short intellectual sounding word meaning: all the stuff you gotta know) is discussed or any class right before a test where potential test questions and general review materials are covered. Skipping or dropping classes can start a vicious cycle. You'll find a natural priority develops for classes you enjoy or are doing well in. Classes in which you do poorly or are behind in, can result in a bad attitude and you may start to skip the class regularly. You skip because you are behind, don't want to be called on, or because you are simply doing poorly and the class lectures bore you. You can swing out of this. Watch how your attitude will change with just one good quiz score, or going into a class lecture prepared and caught up on your reading. There are other things you can do to help yourself swing out of these skipping frenzies. Change your seat in class, prepare very well for just one class, even read ahead. (see chapter on Attitude). Skipping class actually takes approximately four times longer than going to class. Take a look at the **"Blow Off Class vs. Go to Class"** Comparison Chart:

ATTEND CLASS	SKIP CLASS
• Take your own notes, get your own handouts. • Hear the lecture once. • Opportunity to ask questions from the person who knows the answers. • Get your moneys worth since you paid an average of $200 per credit hour.	• Skipping Class (you're obviously doing something important during this time, right?)............................ = **50 minutes.** • Find someone, rap with them for awhile and borrow their notes & handouts...... .... = **30-40 minutes.** • Make copies of notes & handouts........... .... = **25 minutes.** (could vary depending on where Kinkos is or if the school library copiers are working) • Return notes & handout..= **25 minutes.** • Go over notes once since you did not hear lecture....................= **45 minutes.** • Figure out sections of notes, handouts or assignment you do not understand by asking friends or reading text).............. .... =**45-60 minutes.** (Could be longer.)
50 minutes	**4 hours and 20 minutes**

(*Time frames given based on actual experience. Your mileage may vary.)

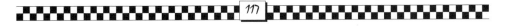

In addition to running the risk that you will not figure out all the notes, etc. it will take four times as long to accomplish what one one hour of class would definitely have accomplished had you attended. What you will definitely accomplish is the following:

- Annoy friends who went to class by borrowing their notes.

- Possibly annoy professor who teaches the class.

- Remove any possibility of effort points to be awarded in the event of a borderline grade dispute.

- Run risk of inferior notes to the ones you could have taken.

- Miss opportunity to ask questions from the only person who definitely knows the material.

- Waste tuition money.

- Become a destitute bum and own a cardboard condo.

More of Celeste and Kippy...

If you are planning on dropping a class with the rationale you will now devote more time to your other courses, be careful. With more free time on your hands you just might waste more time. However if you are seriously overloaded and will maintain a good schedule and study more hours in your remaining classes, then do it. Also, do not fool yourself if you are looking at two bad test grades and you need 99's on the remaining tests to give you a passing grade. You may try talking to the professor about extra credit projects. However, if you are having difficulty keeping up and understanding the current level and caliber of work then extra credit will probably not help your situation.

Talk to your professor first about dropping the class and he or she will tell you if the class becomes more difficult or easy and how much it builds on what you already know or should know. Make sure you know the last date to drop a class and be sure to fill out the necessary paperwork so you do not get an Incomplete or an "F" on your transcripts. You may want to consider either auditing the class or repeating it. You are in college to learn, if you need to take a class over to master the material, then do so!

One rather important place on college campuses which deserves to be mentioned is the library. You know, the place you always tell your parents you are going to and then sneak off into the night and meet your friends and go to the mall or the movies or to a park. Yeah that's right, you know what I am talking about. While in college you won't have to make up this huge story about a research paper and needing to go to the library, because chances are you will really have one or two papers you must get done and they don't get done at the mall. Whatever you do, do not leave your high school without learning how to use the library. Make sure you know how to find a book, a magazine or an article. Yes, you can always ask the librarian to show you, but what happens if there are 25 other students who also did not learn how to use the library in high school, in line in front of you. When you get to your college, check out the library out during your initial exploration and see where the card catalogues are, the microfiche, etc.

Hey, What About. . . ?

More Stuff to Worry About

☐ *Read it. . .* _____

_____

_____

☐ *Check It Out. . .* _____

_____

_____

☐ *Fill It Out. . .* _____

_____

_____

☐ *Think About It. . .* _____

_____

_____

Chapter 15
PROFESSORS

Lets talk about teachers or as we call them in college, professors. In 8,560 words or less I want you to describe your feelings toward professors: (use additional sheets of paper if necessary)

_____

_____

_____

_____

_____

_____

_____

In college, just like in high school, you are going to have the pleasure of being taught by a variety of professors. Each will have his or her own unique personality and style of teaching. You will meet your stereotypical professors who know everything in the world about their subject. They are common in the biology courses. He or she will give you a torture lecture, nonstop, for 12 years just drilling you with information until your head falls off, rolls down the auditorium aisle and explodes. Whereby they continue lecturing, explaining to your headless body the various components of your cerebral hemispheres which now lay before you. Just when you think you have a billionth of a second to catch your breath and get your head back on, your hand cramps up from trying to take notes on additional speed drilling.

How do you handle this type of Terminator Lecturer? It's simple, the same way you handle any Terminator, with cunning and high tech weaponry. A tape recorder will allow you to record the lecture, no matter how intense or rapid its delivery. This allows you to sit back and pay close attention to the material and then after class relisten to the lecture and complete your notes. You will have heard the lecture twice, thus giving you the edge to learn the material thoroughly and be able to graduate in four years with the grades and degree you want while remaining totally cool all throughout and keeping your parents happy etc. . . ., sound familiar.

You will meet the "really get into it" psychology type. If it's a nice day they tell you to "skip class and smell the flowers, life is o.k., let's get into class". Yeah right, try to tell your Intermediate Accounting professor it was such a nice day yesterday you just had to skip his class to smell the flowers.

You will meet professors who do not care if you show up for class and professors who do. Some professors take attendance and base a portion of your grade on your attendance. Different professors require different things, some make you read chapters, do a problem set and hand in your homework. Others simply lecture and expect you to take notes and then know everything. Some give pop quizzes, others do not. Some give a class period for review before a test, others do not. Make sure you understand exactly what is expected and get the run down on a class before you sign up. It is important to get the scoop from older students as to who are the good professors and who are the bad. Remember good doesn't necessarily mean easy and hard does not mean bad. A good professor will make an academically challenging course seem easy while a poor professor will make a true slider course difficult.

Each professor will set up his/her own agenda for the course. They know you probably have five other courses with other assignments, however they still give you whatever reading and homework load they choose. Beat this by staying on top of your reading and homework.

Unfortunately, many times an "us against them attitude" develops between students and professors. Do not be taken up by an age old myth about professors. That is, they are out to get you. I mean think about it. Your professors devote 40 plus hours a week trying to teach you things which are going to help you have a better life. They are spending their lunches, their nights, 9 to 12 months a year helping you learn more so you can get the best out of life. They are dedicated to training you, so someone does not take advantage of you. Think about it!! Is the guy at the "Change your oil and give you a new muffler in 30 seconds for only 2 billion dollars and 99 cents" trying to help you? No, I don't think so. Or the woman who runs your bank, or the guy who sells you those shoes or that backpack, I don't think so. What about the people behind the counter at the burger joint. Are they trying to help you, maybe poison you, but certainly not help you like a dedicated college professor? School is a great time in your life where you have all sorts of people whose job it is to help you help yourself! I realize the mechanics of the educational process, such as exams, term papers and study halls may seem like torture, pain, utter hell (add your own here please....)_____
_____, but the system is designed for you. No other institution in the world is as dedicated to the individual as schooling. So keep in mind professors are on your side and drain their heads of all the knowledge possible, like the professor who drills you until your head falls off.

If you do have a problem with a professor, such as inconsistent grading, unrealistic course loads, problems understanding lectures, then talk to him or her. If serious problems ever surface, such as sexual advances, put downs, blatant grading problems, do not hesitate to talk to the dean or department head for assistance. Find out if other students have had similar problems. Very few professors will not respond to a group of students requesting help or clarifications on grading policies etc.

Check to see how each professor grades. If there are teaching assistants or lab assistants who do the grading, make sure you understand their grading process, and if there are any inconsistencies on any of your papers, homework or tests be sure to check with the professor. (See Chapter 14: The Class)

Hey, What About. . . ?

More Stuff to Worry About

☐ *Read it. . .* _____
_____
_____

☐ *Check It Out. . .* _____
_____
_____

☐ *Fill It Out. . .* _____
_____
_____

☐ *Think About It. . .* _____
_____
_____

Chapter 16

PROCRASTINATION: THE COLLEGE STUDENT'S #1 ENEMY

Did you know, that if you were never to pick up a remote control during college, your chances of graduating in four years double. Occasional MTV sessions to check out the video babes and hunks and your school's sporting events are recommended.

I'm just not into this now, I think I'll check the tube to see what is on.

Tests suck, I hate homework, studying is a drag, term papers really bite the big one, pop quizzes are B.S......!!!!!!!!!!!!!!!!!!!!!!

Please add some of your own:

_____!!!!

_____!!!!

_____!!!!

Thank you. Now that we have that out of our system, we can begin.

Tests and Quizzes:

The greatest fact about tests and quizzes is 99% of the time, teachers actually give you every answer to every question on every test you will ever take. You just need to go to class, especially the one right before the exam, and remember them. The best way to handle tests in college is to handle them before you actually have to take one. That is, stay caught up on your material and study until you know and understand what will be covered. The chapter on scheduling, along with the sections below dealing with studying, will help you deal with tests and quizzes before you have to take them.

By knowing your material and allowing time for a CRP (Casual Review Period), you will go into your tests calm and confident. When you are not ready for a test it is then you become nervous, confused, uptight, wanting to vomit, drop the class and drop out. Try to avoid cramming and all nighters. Make sure you begin to review early, at least two weeks before a test. Mark down a review schedule on your calendar, put a sign on your ceiling or get a tattoo, whatever it takes, and review previously covered chapters on a casual CRP, non rush basis.

Think about something you know how to do well. Let's say taking a jump shot, adjusting your stereo sound to perfection, kicking a soccer ball, combing your hair just right (that never happens), baiting a hook, washing your car, whatever . . . These are things you just do because you know how to and, they are almost second nature, with no pressure. You should prepare for tests until you reach the same No Pressure Knowledge about the material as you would with something you do extremely well. Achieving NPK is not easy. You must stay up on your work in every class, everyday, every week, every month and every semester. Do your problem sets until you not only get through them, but, until you understand why you got through them. Be sure you study both your textbook, class notes and handouts. Usually these will cover the exact same material, but not always. Whatever you do, do not miss the review class right before a test! You hopefully will have started your review process two weeks prior, and professors give great hints as to what is on the test during the last few classes.

The best way to take any college exam or quiz is to be ready.

R = Read the instructions carefully. Ask the professor if they are unclear in any way.

E = Evaluate the questions and time needed. Reread questions and be sure you understand exactly what is asked. Write down outlines for any essay questions and knock-off any easy multiple choice or fill in the blank.

A = Address the questions you know. Answer as completely and as legibly as possible. If there is no penalty, guess on questions you do not know.

D = Details: Fill in additional details on your answers. Other questions on the test probably sparked your recall on some points you left out. If time allows review questions and fill in more detail.

Y = Yo, that was so easy, we did not even need "y".

Sometimes tests will not seem fair and even with all the preparation in the world, you find yourself confronted with confusing questions. Some professors in an attempt to compose challenging questions, actually create confusing ones which do not test your knowledge of the subject, but rather, your ability to guess what the professor is trying to ask. If you run across any questions which are unclear, simply ask the teacher to clarify. Do not try to guess at what is being asked and head off writing in the wrong direction. If possible, find some old tests, they are great practice and you will always find a few similar if not identical questions on the test you take. Some teachers keep a file of their old tests at the library. Fraternities and Sororities usually maintain house files, and most older students will have copies to borrow.

Be on the lookout for another problem, this is lack of time. All you can do, is go into a test as prepared as possible and follow the READY guidelines. If the teacher allows you, ask for a little more time and if not, simply mark "time" on the questions you did not answer. If there is no penalty for guessing, any True/False or multiple choice should be answered and any essays should have an outline jotted down and marked "time".

Promising to be a priest or nun if God just lets you pass this test, or praying for a certain essay question to be on the test or promising you will give all your money to the save the artificial turf society are not feasible alternatives to studying. It is really up to you and your own faith to figure out if you should make these heavenly contracts. In addition, if you make these promises and the only essay question you know, does appear on the test, chances are you won't need good test scores in that subject in the monastery, convent or as primary benefactor for the artificial turf foundation.

Pop quizzes. Hey let's be totally honest here, pop quizzes are the worst, "Hey professor why don't you just poke my eyes out with a hot stick and let my brains seap out my charred eye sockets". Pop quizzes are the ultimate weapons professors use to monitor if you are responsibly scheduling yourself and keeping up on material. But hey, you know what, life is one pop quiz after another, so get used to it. If you learned anything in the chapter on scheduling, then you know how to handle it. The best way is to assume every professor, in every class, is going to give you a pop quiz everyday, and so, you study accordingly. So, as opposed to be being bummed out when professors drop an occasional pop quiz on you, you'll be thrilled when the professors do not drop a quiz on you because you will have assumed they are going to. You will actually start to get bummed when they do not throw pop quizzes at you more often. You might even start asking, or even demanding pop quizzes from your teachers. Whoa! That might be taking it too far.

What about test grades. Always on your first test or quiz, especially if you are not happy with your grade, check with your professor to see why you received the grade. Reviewing a test is important to help you learn what you apparently did not, and gives you an idea how this particular professor grades. So after you receive a test back, double check the grade and see why you missed what you missed. Be sure you hang on to the tests for final review time.

Whatever you do, don't let one bad test score get you down. If you do poorly on a test, do something you enjoy, go hiking, swimming, play one on one, call a friend, anything to renew your positive attitude. Then, as soon as you can, review your mistakes on the test, possibly with your professor and get yourself back on track with the class. Getting a head start on the next exam's material is a good way to rebound from the depression of a bad score. (See Chapter on Attitude)

Reviewing must become a routine with you. Once every two weeks simply set aside an hour or six and review previously covered material in all your classes. This will alleviate massive cram review sessions before an exam. This is a great discipline to master and really takes the pain out of studying for a test, especially for cumulative finals. (See chapter on Scheduling)

Remember to study all handouts, class notes and text book chapters. You must study all of them, not just read the text book instead of going to class, etc.

Cheating and plagiarism in college. Extremely uncool! If you do it you could be history! You might get away with it, but no matter what, sometime in your life it will catch up with you. You cheating plagiaristic scum bucket!

Writing Papers:

There is one secret to writing papers, whether it is a mega research paper or a one page critique of a reading assignment, which will make the difference between a fun project and a project from hell. Start them the day they are assigned. Yes, force yourself to begin gathering your reference information or to read the assignment, the day the paper is assigned. In addition, for mega papers begin to read at least some of your reference information the first week. By immediately starting your paper you have avoided the one sure way to make your writing assignment pure hell. That is to have to research, write and rewrite a six week paper in five days, or worse yet, five nights.

By starting your paper immediately you have allowed yourself time to do your best and avoided the feeling of dreading to start your paper, since you will have already started it. In addition, this early start will assure an early finish and avoid having to write your paper during midterms, finals or other class wrap up projects that occur at the end of quarters or semesters. By starting your paper right away you also will avoid waiting for common reference material and lines at the copier. And remember, just because you finish your paper early does not mean you have to hand it in early. You do not necessarily want to give your professor his first paper to read when he has a great deal of critical time grading it. Chances are, if you started your paper early, you have given yourself plenty of time to do a quality job.

Another important hint when writing papers is if you are allowed to pick out your own topic, find one you are definitely interested in. Think about it, would you be more enthused about writing a paper on "The cumulative effects of Carbon Dioxide and ultraviolet light on single celled organisms in a petrie dish environment" or "The cumulative effects of pizza and Hawaiian Punch on college freshman in a toga party environment". The latter definitely is more fun to research, however, you probably will not find it as a potential research paper topic choice. Most writing assignments give you a window of subject areas, and within those areas, you can pick a topic. So immediately do some checking at the library for topics which have plenty of information available and find one that interests you.

Here are some thoughts to keep in mind whenever a paper is assigned. Note; there are other methods for writing papers and your counselor, along with the suggested readings below, should provide you with some additional useful information.

1 Your first step is to simply read on the subject. This preliminary reading will help you select a subject and you can then check on available information at your college and local libraries. Preferably skim over several sources of information and determine your topic.

2 Get a three ring binder notebook designated for organizing and writing papers. This "Paper Buster" will allow you to collect your research material and order it in any fashion you want. Make sure it has pockets to stuff in loose material until you punch holes in them. You will organize your notes into a sequence and in a format you understand and is easy to follow. (Call 800-222-6462 for three ring binders made out of recycled paperboard)

3 Definitely use a computer to write the paper. Use a wordprocessor so features such as spell checking and cutting and pasting can be used.

Store one copy of the paper on the harddrive and store one disk copy in your binder. If the computer is not yours, make two disk copies, one for the binder and one for anywhere else but the binder. You can print out hardcopies for storage and proofing whenever you feel it is necessary.

4 Once you have read and researched your topic and organized your notes, then formulate an outline. This should cover main topics you need to include and gives you ideas to begin writing. If possible, this outline should follow an Introduction, Body and Conclusion format or whatever format your professor assigned. Ask your professor to review your outline so you do not waste time going off in the wrong direction.

5 Write a first draft. Do not worry about further organization, grammar, too much information, or too little, just write what you know.

6 Fill in or extract additional information and polish existing points. Rewrite and rearrange (cut and paste) to further organize and complete the paper.

7 Do not look at the paper or at anything to do with the paper for two or three days. Then, with a clear head, complete a thorough reading. Edit as necessary.

8 Have a friend proofread it. Polish if necessary.

9 Spell Check one final time!!!!!!!! Utilize Grammar checker if available!!!!!!

10 Print it, make back up copies (disk and hardcopy). Prepare to hand in.

11 **Hang and have some fun!**

Reading:

One great rule of thumb is to complete all reading assignments prior to the lecture. It makes the lecture easier to follow and note taking is not as difficult. In addition, you will be able to ask the professor to clarify any points you do not understand. The best thing you can do to improve your reading skills is to read. Over the summer try to read at least four books, preferably more. Although most academic types would recommend reading literary masterpieces such as The Odyssey or Romeo and Juliet and this is great advice, reading anything is better than nothing. Read a "How to Fly Fish" book or a novel about a foreign country you have always wanted to visit. It is important to practice your reading. Taking a speed reading course can also be beneficial.

Problem sets:

First of all, let's not call them problems, let's call them questions. Most courses routinely use questions or exercises to teach concepts discussed in class lectures. Courses, such as Physics, Calculus, Accounting and Public Finance are really based on using concepts and formulas to solve problems. Whether it is an Accounting question on Debits and Credits or a Calculus question, such as . . .such as . . .aaaaaaahh . . . well such as . . . um, actually I do not remember any of my Calculus questions. Oh well, you get the point.

When you are confronted with homework questions try to address them immediately after they are assigned. So get your behind into the "Optima Study Position" at the "Optima Study Place" as soon as possible after the homework is assigned. (Look ahead for more on the Optima Study Position and Place)

Your first step in dominating this homework set is to not grab a blank sheet of paper and read Question #1 as fast as you can and try to answer it. First, you should read carefully and review the material the questions cover. This includes any reading to be completed and then any sample exercises covered in class. When you understand the material and logic behind the sample exercises, then start question #1. If you try to answer the questions before you fully understand the concepts or sample exercises, chances are, you will become frustrated, waste time and get a major bad attitude. Trying to figure out questions, by reading only certain sections of the lesson, and basically on a "figure out as you go basis" is the wrong way.

You will see a major difference by first understanding the material and then trying any homework sets. The questions will certainly seem easier and you will complete them in less time. Following the pointers given in the chapter on The Class dealing with paying attention and taking notes will definitely shorten the prehomework review time, and you will develop a positive attitude toward homework questions.

Where to Study: Optima Study Place and Optima Study Position

Whether it is in your dorm room, frat or sorority room, on campus, at the library, or in an empty classroom, find yourself a low traffic, low distraction Optima Study Place. This will be a particular table or study booth in the library. It might be an empty classroom or in your own room with your neatly arranged desk whereby you can study for long durations without distraction. You need a "Primo study area, no way to chill, guaranteed to learn study space." It should be a large table no recliner, foot rest etc.. Secondly, have a "2nd wind, could chill" location such as a couch with a coffee table for a change of pace. If you have difficulty staying awake while you study, try a drafting table and study standing. Who knows, maybe you will become another Winston Churchill who wrote many of his books standing up or in the bathtub. Then again maybe you have no desire to be a dead, British, former Prime Minister.

In any selected Optima Study Place you should configure yourself in the Optima Study Position. This studying layout is a perfect composition of book placement, notebook angling, beverage/munchy supply and access, calculator positioning and writing utensil selection, all orchestrated for the sole purpose of efficient study material placement and can only be ineffective if you forget the most important design factor. This is to put your head down in your book and study.

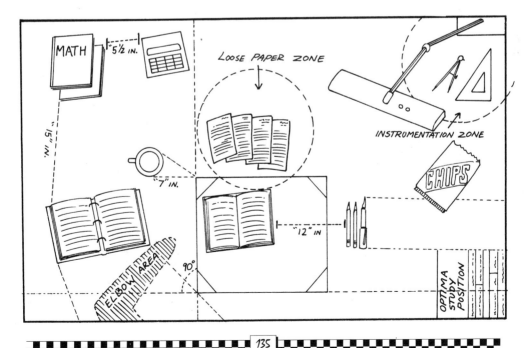

Watch out for social centers. Unfortunately, the historic center of knowledge, the "library" is also the social center. Many students go through the ritual of setting a study station or library base camp (LBC). They open their books into the Optima Study Position only to leave them to collect dust as they scope out who else has set up LBC's in the library. Also, the cafeteria is a major social center and, if you are not careful, you might end up taking two hour lunches and dinners that will literally "eat" up much of your study time. Studies have been done and show it is good to study in the room where you will take a particular test. Campuses are full of empty classrooms at night and professors and \or janitorial staff are usually willing to make these available to students for studying. In fact, sit at the same desk you plan on sitting at during the test. Do not try and study in bed or with a TV or stereo turned on. Listening to music is definitely not good for your analytical, logic and memorization classes. I have a friend who swore the only way he could study was with Bruce Springsteen's "Born to Run" on his head phones, and drumming with two pencils as he read. He always studied in this fashion, always, and I do not think he passed any of his classes, but he did know the words to all of the Boss's songs.

Study Breaks:

Your first study break will always be right after a class. Make it short. Take a walk to the library or your study area and then force yourself to study for a least 35-50 minutes immediately after a class. Use this time to review material, recopy notes from your last class or begin reading assigned material. If you have two or three classes in a row try to do some form of exercise (racquetball, swimming, running . . .) after the classes and then sit down and begin your studying. (See chapter on Scheduling)

How long you study in one sitting is your decision. Try to sit down and study for a least as long as your class period, say 50 minutes to an hour and a half. When you need to take a break, always try to get some form of exercise. Take a walk outside around the library or wherever. If you want to talk with a friend then both of you go for a walk.

It is important to add some variety to your studying. Believe it or not, group studying or studying with someone else is a great way to add variety unless it always turns into a major rap session, or worse yet, a huge party with rock music, pizza, beverages of choice, more pizza, five zazillion of your closest friends, more beverages of choice and no books to be seen. Hey that doesn't sound too bad!

Studying with someone else allows you question and answer periods and an opportunity to compare notes. Playing teacher is a good group study game. I don't mean you take turns acting like a dork and making life miserable by lecturing at your friends and giving them so much homework they are never seen or heard from again. It simply means you find a classroom and one person goes to the board and explains some part of the material to the others. Everyone else has the opportunity to add information and ask questions. Take turns doing this until all the test material has been covered. It is a great game since it makes studying fun, gives everyone an opportunity to stand up and recite important material, and a group of students working together will assure all relevant material is covered.

All nighters are not a good idea. In fact, allnighters, unless they involve good friends, beverages of choice and a twister game, should be avoided at all costs. Studies show the refreshed human mind can absorb much more material in half the time in the morning as a tired mind can late at night. Does this mean if you are confronted with a situation where you have a test tomorrow and have not read any of the chapters it covers you should just blow it off and flunk. No way!!! Get your buns in the Optima Study Place and Position and learn as much as you can. However be fair to yourself. Get at least four hours of sleep and hopefully you will pass the test and be smarter for having gone through the pain of the all nighter.

Grades:

Sorry, there are no mystery formulas or secret hints to help you get good grades. It is true you must pay attention to your grades if you are trying to get into medical school or law school or other graduate programs. However, if you just manage your classes you will not have the headache of getting behind or poor grades. It is truly easier to do things right then to do them wrong. If you follow the advice in this book to the best of your ability and apply yourself, grades should follow. All professors have their own grading schemes and methods. The best way to handle each of them is to not worry about getting a 76% vs. an 82%, rather concentrate on learning the material taught and getting the most out of every class, test, lecture, paper and homework assignment. Do not get caught in thinking a C or D or even an F is going to wreck your life because it will not!

This is an important section so I hope you paid attention, or even read it twice. Here are some additional books and activities you should check out over the summer or in your spare time. Yeah I know what your saying, "like I don't have anything better to do"!

1. "Dancing with your Books, The Zen Way of Studying" by J.J. Gibbs. Published by the Penguin Group.

2. Memorization Book such as "The Memory Book" by Harry Lorayne. Published by New American Library, a division of Penguin Books

3. "How to Study in College" by Walter Punk. Published by Houghton Mifflin Company.

4. Typing or Computer Course if you have not already taken one.

5. Speed Reading Course

Hey, What About. . . ?

More Stuff to Worry About

☐ *Read it. . .* _____

_____

_____

☐ *Check It Out. . .* _____

_____

_____

☐ *Fill It Out. . .* _____

_____

_____

☐ *Think About It. . .* _____

_____

_____

NOTES

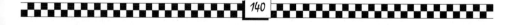

Chapter 18
PARTYING

"Party Hardy Marty . . ." *spoken by Bill Murray in the movie SCROOGED*

Drinking & Drugs

For some of you, your high school social scene served as a testing ground for trying and/or using alcohol, pot and other drugs. For some of you, college will serve as a testing ground for trying and/or using alcohol, pot and other drugs. At almost every college or university, you are going to be confronted with this and depending on what you learned about drinking and drugs in high school, you will be forced to deal with this situation. Your starting point to deal with this issue is to know the legal drinking age (either 19 or 21) in your school's state and to compare that number with your own age. If that number is less than or equal to your age, then you can legally drink if you so choose. If that number is greater than your age, then you cannot legally, and should not illegally, drink alcohol. I know what you're saying, "Everybody drinks man, who are you kidding, telling me to check the legal age?" First of all, who wants to be just like everybody else, and secondly, if you won't check it, there are plenty of other people from police officers to servers and bouncers at bars, who will. Being caught with a fake I.D. or getting served while underage is not only going to mess you up, but you could also cause employees their jobs or a restaurant or bar to lose its license. Not exactly a great way to make friends.

You will find alcohol at almost every collegiate social function. You will certainly find it at every pub, restaurant or bar. And you probably will find it in most dorm, frat and sorority refrigerators. I am sure you have been told by some elder authority figure at least once already to learn your limits and drink socially, keeping in mind the health aspects of abuse. But what exactly does it mean? It means, if you can legally drink and choose to drink alcohol, do not drink just to get hammered. Believe it or not, it is not cool, attractive or even fun, to drink till you fall over and puke on yourself or on somebody else (so I've heard). When going to a party, football game or out for the night, if you choose to drink beer or other alcoholic drinks, simply pace yourself. Have one or two alcoholic drinks instead of eight, or drink soda instead, and always eat something. You will find you will be able to party longer since you won't get as tired so quickly. In addition, you will be able to get up early the next morning feeling good, because you will not have a hang over. All a hangover is, is your body telling you, "Thanks for poisoning me last night, don't mind me pounding your head and trashing your stomach, it's just the old kidneys cannot process all of this alcohol, but if you just continue to get drunk often enough, then I promise you I won't bother you anymore, I'll just shut down."

More of Steve and Kelmar...

Don't be such a weak loser that you cannot tell someone no! This goes for drinking, drinking games, and drugs. If someone gives you a bad time about choosing not to do drugs or drinking, then they are not worth hanging around. You should be able to hang out with people who drink, even if you do not. Telling your friends you do not care for a drink or a hit might be uncomfortable at first. They might try to persuade you and act disappointed if you do not join in. Sometimes the thing to do is talk to your friends, say the next day, when they are sober and simply tell them you do not like to drink or smoke pot, or whatever, and it is no big deal and you still hope they want to include you in their social functions, if you want to be included. Nine times out of ten, in this setting, your real friends will be just that, your friends. The good thing about college is usually all parties are mixers where some students drink and some do not. It's entirely up to you. You can drink a nonalcoholic beer, or an orange juice, nobody has to know what you are drinking.

Do not, under any circumstances, let yourself or your friends drive drunk. Never, not even once. There are certainly many stupid things you can and probably will do, in college, but do not let this be one of them. It is illegal, and a first offense in almost every state will result in a fine, and a suspended license, even with probation. That is the good side. The bad side is you could kill or maim you and your friends. Not exactly the ideal memory to have about your fun college days. There are two good ideas to help prevent this. I suggest you get them implemented when you go to college if they are not already.

 When you go out, if anyone in your group is going to drink alcohol, then always assign a Designated Driver. This person drives and does not have even one drop of alcohol or other drugs. Don't worry, the designated driver does not miss one second of the party, he or she is there from beginning to end, they have a ball.

 Create a **Cab Tab Fund** on your dorm floor or at your Frat or Sorority. This fund has money available to pay for cabs which are sent out for people who should not be driving. The Resident Assistants or house officers can manage the program for your floors and houses, making sure someone is always around to assist with driving, arriving taxi's or taking calls from groups who have encountered a self-inflicted stranding. Everyone pitches in and the users of the service reimburse the fund every time they use it.

This same idea applies to drug use also. Possession of pot, cocaine, crack, LSD or other drugs is a definite fine and possible jail time. Trafficking a controlled substance is a definite fine and definite jail time. The mere quantity of drugs in your possession can make the difference between possession and trafficking. That's the good news. The bad news is, drugs like crack, cocaine and LSD can kill you and your friends, quickly, first time, goodbye!!

There is a tendency when in college, especially freshman year to be swallowed up by all the partying opportunities. There are happy hours, noon hours, post games, pregames, Togas, Costume Parties, Monday Night Football, Tuesday Night 2 for 1's, Wednesday Night Hump Day, Thursday Night Ladies Night and of course the Weekend which at some colleges, actually begins on Wednesday. Fraternities and sororities throw parties to get ready for a party, A Preparty Preparation Party. Partying too much is one of the most, if not the most, common cause of poor academic performance. You must learn to control your partying or to say it a better way, schedule your socializing opportunities. The fact of the matter is, the more you study, the more your can really party. People think these two activities are inversely related, however, they are not. If you stay up on your studies and make use of your day hours through the scheduling tips I have outlined and utilize Quality Study Time, then you can experience more Quality Leisure Time. It is only when you waste time during the day and throughout a given week you find yourself not able to or feeling guilty about going out. Here are a few tips from the **Party Quick Reference Guide** to help you party more.

 Make good use of your time by following the scheduling and study tips. (See Chapters #12, #13, #15).

 Only attend QLT parties. If you have things you should be doing, chances are, you won't enjoy yourself anyway.

 Do not be concerned about getting out early to party. Prior to every party get into the habit of studying for 45-50 minutes. Chances are you will not have missed anything!

 When you do go out, if you drink at all, drink in moderation and always try to eat something if you are drinking.

 Exercise your lazy butt! This will keep your energy level up and give you greater party endurance.

 Pick your parties. Not every party is worth going to and you can be sure there will always be another one.

Hey, What About. . . ?

More Stuff to Worry About

☐ *Read it.* . . _____
_____
_____

☐ *Check It Out.* . . _____
_____
_____

☐ *Fill It Out.* . . _____
_____
_____

☐ *Think About It.* . . _____
_____
_____

NOTES

Chapter 19

RELATIONSHIPS, DATING & MEETING PEOPLE

Yes, I know what you're thinking, you are asking yourself, "Does this chapter tell me what to do about going to a different college then my current boyfriend or girlfriend, and will we be able to stay together and later marry or will he or she find someone they like better and what if they do and forget I ever existed and will I vomit, roll up in a ball and die if it happens?" The answer is yes. Not yes to will you vomit, roll up in a ball and die, but yes, I am going to tell you what to do about it.

The answer to, "What can you do about it?" is really very simple. There is absolutely nothing you can do about it, so do not spend so much as a second worrying about it. Nobody can predict what will happen to a relationship during college. Here are a few simple pointers you should remember as you near the beginning of your college separation:

1 You and your boyfriend or girlfriend have an identically equal chance of meeting someone else during your college years, unless, one of you goes to the convent and the other to the French Foreign Legion.

2 The best thing for a young relationship is to have both people go out and meet as many other people as they can. Would you want someone with you only because you are the only person they know?

3 The best way to handle the separation which occurs during college is to try and leave on a good note with your boyfriend or girlfriend. Enjoy your high school days and summer together and do not worry about what will happen later.

4 Plan on and verbally agree to see other people during your first year away at college. In this way no one is cheating on the other because you both agreed to it. This does not imply that either of you feel any different toward one another, it just means you are mature and being fair to yourself and to your boyfriend or girlfriend.

5 Be honest and stay in touch. Write letters and call your boyfriend and girlfriend. Do not interrogate each other about, "Who did you go out with last weekend?" or "What does your date to the dance look like?" or "Did you kiss him or her?" If by chance you did kiss him or her you are dead meat anyway!!

6 Realize there is nothing you can do if your feelings or your boyfriend or girlfriends' feelings change. You cannot change it by worrying, writing everyday, eating, not eating, yelling, screaming, spitting, sleeping, dancing or partying. The best thing you can do is follow #7 and I guarantee things will work out for the best.

7 The best thing you can do for a high school relationship while in college, is to take great care of yourself. Get the most out of your classes, stay in great shape, and enjoy your new friends. Only by doing this will you truly do the best for yourself and your high school sweetheart in the long run.

Since I have completely blown apart your worries about being separated from your high school sweetheart, let's talk about your other major concern;

Meeting people:

The great thing about college is there is no better environment in the world set up in such a way, that you are forced to meet so many people on a daily basis. You have groups of people meeting every single day, morning, noon and night in classes, meetings, sessions, lunches, dinners, happy hours, games, pregames, post games, parties, concerts, walks, runs, religious services, seminars, lines, study breaks, spring breaks, coffee breaks...................on and on and on. Obviously, if you have chosen to enter the Greek system, you have social events planned for you on a regular basis. This lifestyle is very conducive to meeting new people. If you have chosen not to be part of a fraternity or sorority, then select organizations or activities which interest you and join them.

You will meet many new people during college, whether you want to or not. Although you should be outgoing to meet people, it is a good idea when surrounded with new faces to simply listen more then you talk. This way you can sort out the losers, jerks, scums (feel free to fill in your own_____) from the cool people. The law of averages states, for every 100 cool persons, there is at least one loser, jerk or scum. Avoid this person!! Obviously, one of the greatest places to meet people is in the classroom. It can lead to studying together which is a great way to get to know a person. Be cautious when meeting people. Do not run off with strangers at any given time. It is best to meet people and get to know them in public places first. See if you have any mutual acquaintances, chances are you probably do. Remember, quality not quantity is the rule for friends. I would rather be the most unknown person in the Campus Save the Whales Organization than, the most popular, in the Beat Baby Seals To Death with a Club Club.

Dating:

By first getting together at public parties or by doubling with friends you can avoid potentially dangerous situations. Date rape or being pressured into taking drugs are often, but not always, the result of being in the wrong place at the wrong time. There is no excuse for people to force themselves onto another. If you are the victim of any sexual harassment or rape, you should contact the police immediately, and pursue your legal options to the maximum! Only in this way will you assure that the assailant is punished and that your own mental well being will be protected by the knowledge you did what was necessary to right the wrong.

What happens if in college you meet someone you like very much and would like to date, but they do not like you or just want to be friends? Well, obviously you should completely freak out and fling yourself from the tallest structure on campus. Right? Wrong! You should fling them from the tallest structure on campus? Right? Well . . .Wrong! First you should vocalize to close friends your displeasure at the fact that this person does not worship you. This will get the matter off your chest and should prompt your friends to cheer you up. Then you should follow rule #7 from above and realize some relationships will not work out. Do not think there is only one Mr. or Mrs. Right for you. If someone is not giving you the consideration and time you feel you deserve or are willing to give them, find someone who will. Once again, keep in mind rule #7 from above, take care of yourself first. This does not mean be inconsiderate of others, just help yourself first, so you can help others later. There will come a time when you will want to share your life more fully with another person.

Why one night stands are a mistake:

I know there are some of you tracking down all copies of <u>How To Get Into and Graduate From College in Four Years</u> and ripping out this section, but, I at least hope you read it before you do.

If this section were written so it said what you wanted to hear, it would go something like this. When you get to college do absolutely anything your hormones and body desire, sleep with anyone who says hello to you and their friends, take part in every kinky sex act asked of you and generally have a happy yet responsible sex life. Now, if this section said what we all know to be true, it would sound like this. True, during college you will run across many new and exciting people whom you will become attracted to. College is the time to meet people and naturally you will embark on relationships. Take the time to really know your girlfriends and boyfriends and this will lead to healthier and happier relationships, and in addition, it truly does result in the most fulfilling experience for two people.

If you really are interested in someone and want them to return this interest, then a one night stand will just lead to each of you wondering what type of a person the other really is. The fact of the matter is, if a person is truly interested in you for more than just a one night stand, they will wait. They will call you, they will talk to you and they will give you the respect and courtesy you deserve, and they will wait!

O.k., here goes, here comes the word you do not want to hear...

ready........are you ready..........seeettt ....Abstinence.......uughhhh!!!!!!!!!!!
(uughhh = sound that Charlie Brown makes when Lucy pulls the football away at the last second and he misses kicking it and falls flat on his back in a pile of dust). Abstinence is really not so bad. It limits your exposure to sexually transmitted diseases, prevents unwanted pregnancies and should not prevent intimacy with your girlfriend or boyfriend. In addition, you can always go forward when you decide, but you can never go back.

I know what your saying, "What happens if my girlfriend or boyfriend and I both want to have sex?" "What if we are sure we are ready and need to express our love by this intimate act". Well, if you have decided you are ready for that level of intimacy, then whatever you do, practice the safest sex possible. Practice it for your own health, practice it for the life of a child. The decision to practice safe sex is a lot easier than the decision to have a child, an abortion, get married or not, putting a child up for adoption, select an AIDS treatment, etc. If you are unsure about any topics concerning safe sex and contraception, then ask your school nurse to give you some information and study it!!!!! Do not listen to any brain dead fools who say brilliant things like "I never use a rubber" or "Contraception is up to my girlfriend". If you get to the point in a relationship where you have decided to make a commitment to someone and believe you both are ready to have sex, then you should have discussed what precautions you are going to take and plan on sharing the responsibilities. Responsibilities are: the cost of birth control, the risk of a pregnancy, and the obligations of intimacy.

Keep in mind as far as one night stands go, both young men and women get to a point in their life where they do not want nor are they looking for, "I got through college on my back, Betty.", or "Give me anything with a skirt, Skip.", but they are attracted to genuine people who strike up relationships based on respect and attraction towards a particular person. Patience pays here.

Friends:

Support your friends and have only friends who support you. It seems sometimes your friends are not always on your side. They might try to keep you down, not wanting you to do things you excel at or enjoy. If this seems to be the case with a friend of yours, simply tell him or her you do not appreciate their lack of support or enthusiasm for your successes. A success of a true friend is truly your success as well. Be happy for their successes. Remember compete against the books not against your friends.

Hey, What About. . . ?

More Stuff to Worry About

☐ Read it. . . _____
_____
_____

☐ Check It Out. . . _____
_____
_____

☐ Fill It Out. . . _____
_____
_____

☐ Think About It. . . _____
_____
_____

NOTES

Chapter 20

PARENTS AND/OR PARENTAL FIGURES

One of the major contributors without a doubt, to growth in college stems from the fact you are away from your parents or parental figures. (assuming you do go away to school or at least live outside your parents home during the college experience) You are now free to make your own decisions regarding studying, sleep, eating, partying, finances, etc. Decisions between running over to the library to review some notes and running over to the pub for a game of pool will have to be confronted daily and nightly. If you have aspirations to be a drunken pool shark, then you should opt for the bar. If you have aspirations to be a self supporting human with a job and a life, then you should go to the library.

Although you might think parents are clueless to what it is like to be a teenager these days, they understand more than you realize. Before you begin your college days be sure to tap your parents unlimited sources of knowledge and wisdom about experiences they had or did not have in college. (This goes for your counselors and teachers at high school also.) If you don't find the conversations very enlightening at least, I am sure, you will find them humorous. With this in mind, at the end of the chapter there are coupons redeemable for $5.00 by your parents or parental figure, for you taking the time to ask them one question; "What is the one piece of advice you can give me about going to college". This one piece of advice probably will turn into a three hour mini series entitled "Gone with the Grades". Certain restrictions apply. Such as, if your parents don't go for it. If that is the case, just tell them fine, if your college career isn't worth $5.00 bucks then you'll just hang out at home for another four years and have all of your friends over every night whose parents also did not think a discussion on college was worth $5.00.

It's very important you openly discuss with your parents what you really want to study. (See section on Majors) Do not try and study to be a doctor just because your dad is a doctor and he wants you also to be one. However you should listen very carefully to what your parents have to say in terms of studies and careers. They wouldn't tell you to go into something unless they felt it was an enriching and lucrative career path. You rarely hear parents say to their sons and daughters, "Hey Ted or Tammy, why don't you think about majoring in "Cordless High Altitude Balloon Bungee Jumping". (A very tedious major. Lots of study time and only one final exam with no retakes) The last thing parents want is their kids to be back at home at age 27, with no education, merely a financial and mental burden, eating them out of house and home, and not even willing to take the trash out. I know this, just ask my parents how they feel.

Your parents want you to succeed more than you probably do, so listen to them and discuss all your goals and thoughts on going to college and potential careers.

Your mother and I would like to see you make something of yourselves. . .

Here are a few things you should remember about typical parents once their siblings go off to school. These behavioral patterns are easy to recognize and should not be misinterpreted as parents being uncool. Rather, these behaviors demonstrate that parents are just trying to get the best for their kids.

Pattern #1:   Parents feel if you are away they must get their lectures in during short phone conversations and make them more intense since you are not always around for those **"saturation lectures"**. I guarantee you "long distance is the next best thing". Parents can give a pretty good lecture over the telephone lines. Do not be alarmed. They are just trying to help by getting a lot of lecture in a short time frame.

Pattern #2:   Parents tend to focus on grades as the overall indicator of how their sons and daughters are doing in college. Get used to it. Unfortunately so does everyone else in the world.

Pattern #3:   Parents think if they keep you broke in college, whether intentionally or not, you won't be able to do anything but study. This paternal financial power move is best countered by getting a part time job which gives you a little extra money, plus forces you to schedule your studies better.

Pattern 4#:   Remember when you were younger and you tried to talk your parents into letting you do something (like stay up until 11:00 o'clock on a school night or go to an R rated movie) and you would tell them that Adolph or Adella's parents let them stay up until 11:00pm or their parents take them to R movies. Well, college is a time when your parents might let you know about one of their friend's sons or daughters, who are on the varsity tennis team, are majoring in Electrical Engineering and are getting a 3.98 GPA. Do not be alarmed or discouraged, they are simply trying to motivate you. Parents, like students, have a natural tendency to compete and compare their children with other parents' children. Just keep in mind the Major Maxim #3 "Support your friends, be happy for their successes. Compete against the books not your friends or other students". If it really gets on your nerves you can use the same old logic they would counter with when you were a kid. Just tell them, "Well, I am not Adolph or Adella", or "if Adolph jumped off a bridge should I" might well serve to counter here. Or it just might get your car keys taken away.

$5 **$5**

COUPON

This coupon is redeemable for $5.00 by any parent or parental figure when presented by a potential college student who asks "What is the one piece of advice you can give me about going to college". To be redeemed the student must sit and listen to any and all advice by the parental figure no matter how long it takes. Parental figure, upon completion of lecture must promptly pay student.

Parents: Under no circumstances can this coupon be sent to Westgate Publishing for $5.00. You should be thrilled at the opportunity to discuss your kid's college plans. Besides, they would have got $5.00 out of you today anyway. So what's new.

$5 **$5**

$5 **$5**

COUPON

This coupon is redeemable for $5.00 by any parent or parental figure when presented by a potential college student who asks "What is the one piece of advice you can give me about going to college". To be redeemed the student must sit and listen to any and all advice by the parental figure no matter how long it takes. Parental figure, upon completion of lecture must promptly pay student.

Parents: Under no circumstances can this coupon be sent to Westgate Publishing for $5.00. You should be thrilled at the opportunity to discuss your kid's college plans. Besides, they would have got $5.00 out of you today anyway. So what's new.

$5 **$5**

$5 **$5**

COUPON

This coupon is redeemable for $5.00 by any parent or parental figure when presented by a potential college student who asks "What is the one piece of advice you can give me about going to college". To be redeemed the student must sit and listen to any and all advice by the parental figure no matter how long it takes. Parental figure, upon completion of lecture must promptly pay student.

Parents: Under no circumstances can this coupon be sent to Westgate Publishing for $5.00. You should be thrilled at the opportunity to discuss your kid's college plans. Besides, they would have got $5.00 out of you today anyway. So what's new.

$5 **$5**

Chapter 21
BREAKS

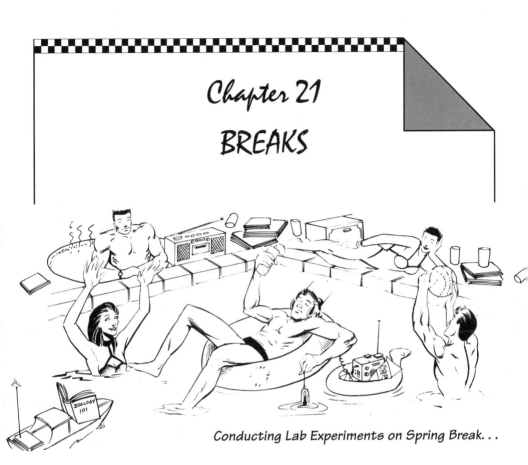

Conducting Lab Experiments on Spring Break. . .

The Ballad of Spring Break

There once was a boy named Martin
Who took his books on break to be a spartan
Little did he know
Once away from his college all covered in snow
He forgot all about his books, hung out, partied all night and got a sun burn.

DO NOT TAKE YOUR BOOKS ON BREAKS. You are not going to study anyway. I actually took a Zoology & Chemistry book on a spring break to Phoenix, Arizona. I was visiting my brother who went to ASU. I thought I could study for some upcoming exams. Yeah. I studied wildlife alright, all different species, blondes, brunettes, even the elusive red head. As far as organic compounds, sure . . . Coors, Budweisers and Miller Light. I even did some lab experiments. I mixed Coors light with extra-spicy cheese nachos, let them sit in my stomach as I sat in 90 degree celsius temperatures for 5 hours, occasionally submersing myself in 78 degree slightly chlorinated water and centrifuging myself by spinning on a Captain Nimo raft laying in the pool. I would have published the results of the test but I do not remember them. I have to admit, that experiment beat the hell out of watching litmus paper turn colors!

Take advantage of your breaks, if you really think you can get some reviewing time in on a plane or something fine, but do not try to use your breaks as catch up time. Remember QLT is so important and it results in very productive QST.

Take full advantage of your breaks. Travel, go home with new friends, go home to old friends or just plain go. Do not use breaks as a catch up time. Hopefully, you have scheduled yourself and will stay on top of your studies.

Try to set goals for going certain places on your breaks. They can serve as nice rewards for staying disciplined all quarter or semester.

Ways to use your books on breaks. . .

Hey, What About. . . ?

More Stuff to Worry About

☐ Read it. . . _____
_____
_____

☐ Check It Out. . . _____
_____
_____

☐ Fill It Out. . . _____
_____
_____

☐ Think About It. . . _____
_____
_____

NOTES

Chapter 22

PROCRASTINATION: THE COLLEGE STUDENT'S #1 ENEMY

Yes, meet the college students number one enemy! It can disguise its hideous omnipresent self in all forms, as a party, as a telephone call, as fast food, even as one of your friends! Beware though, the result is always the same. First it distracts you, then it takes your discipline, it can even rob you of your money, and worst of all, it can leave you behind and stressed to the max!!! The only defense against this omnivorous plague which roams college campus' day and night hunting and devouring weak students who fall prey to its traps, is to conquer it before it conquers you!!!!!!!!!!!

Yes, now that you are going to college, you will not have mommy or daddy to protect your weak little self from this creature by making you stay home after dinner forcing you to do your homework. And, if you think you have been clever by telling your parents that you are going to the library and then actually going out with your friends, or by blowing reading assignments off and buying Cliff notes, then you are sure to come face to face with this drooling, butt breathed, alien look alike award winner, scum oozing demon!!!!

And don't think your friends and peers will save you! More than likely they will toss you into its jaws laughing as it crunches your bones and tears your flesh, ripping your books from your hands and leaving you behind in your studies, depressed and extremely uptight about trying to cram a billion years of studying and homework into one night!

So, are you getting the point here? Procrastination is definitely one of your biggest enemies in college and it does lurk around every corner day and night. Putting things off until the last minute will give you an Major Bad Attitude (Remember Chapter #10). It forces you to rush through work and when test time comes you will not be in a good position to review. When you do procrastinate, and finally decide to start studying, you find

yourself having to read chapters, understand them, get questions asked, answer things you don't understand, do problem sets, learn problem sets and then review the material, all in a very short time. The transition from reading to understanding to knowing takes time.

A student will rationalize him or herself into extraordinary study and comprehension abilities. A person will convince himself he can digest a large amount of knowledge and material the night before a test. For example:

It is Friday afternoon and you have a test next Thursday. You say to yourself you have plenty of time to prepare for it. However note your current position in the class. You are 4 chapters behind in the reading, the test will cover 6, so you have a total of six to read. You have 6 problem sets which need to be worked and understood. So you say to yourself O.K., I'll read 2 chapters a day, starting Saturday because of course its Friday afternoon and nothing is going to get read today. This means by Tuesday you should have all chapters read. Now don't forget about the problem sets. You have to spend time after you read each chapter to do a problem set. And then starting Tuesday you must review making sure you understand all the problems and can successfully work them on your own so that by Thursday you are ready for the test.

So here it is Saturday morning and you're about to begin your study agenda for this one test.

SATURDAY

11:45am: Well before you even start your studying you already encounter a problem... It is not Saturday morning rather Saturday afternoon because you went out late last night and are just getting up.

12:30pm: You finish taking a shower, shaving whatever (studies indicate the average college freshman takes anywhere from 22 minutes to 1 hour and ten minutes to get out of bed and functioning in the morning. This figure varies depending on the (3) WATSWAYENFORYA factors, one factor, the circumstances awaiting the college freshman when he awakes, calculus test, intramural football game, aerobics, work, absolutely nothing, factor two, day of the week Monday morning versus Sunday morning. Factor three, what you did the night before. INTERESTING ENOUGH it was found the average freshman gets out of bed 4.2 times faster when there is absolutely nothing waiting for him then if there is a calculus test. The author of these studies has not been identified and is probably sleeping right now.)

12:35pm: You call a few friends or go to their dorm and you end up bs.ing about the night before.

1:15pm: You all realize you missed breakfast and lunch at the cafeteria and decide to go grab a bite out.. But before you go you have to wait for a few other people to go through their wake up rituals, scrape some money up, make a few phone calls, get a few phone calls, talk about the night out and then decide to go eat.

1:40pm: You finally take off to grab some food and although you are not making a conscious decision to save time, you probably go to a fast food place. So you hit one of the more notorious fast food grease joints.

2:30pm: After your high energy meal it's back to campus to hit the books. You go back to your sorority, fraternity or dorm room and plop down on your bed to let your food digest (I got news for you, that food NEVER digests.)

3:00pm: You gather your notes and books and it is off to the library. The walk to the library is about 5-6 minutes however you run into some friends and talk for about 5 minutes and they tell you about a party tonight, but you tell them you are studying and they laugh. You now remember you have to swing by a classmates to pick up some notes from a lecture you missed. This trip takes an extra 25 minutes because you have to make copies of them since they also need to study for the test.

At 10 minutes to 4:00pm you make it to the library.

4:00pm: You of course run into several more friends, one classmate who needs the notes you just received, one classmate who has other notes you need and by the time you get a pop and find a table setting up your LBC (Library Base Camp) it is

4:30pm: You sit down and spread your books and notes into the "Optima Study Position" and you are now ready to begin studying on Saturday just four days before your six chapter test covering one and a half months of material.

At 5:30pm: It's time for dinner and since you missed breakfast and lunch and have no more dinero for dinner you head to find some friends and go to the cafeteria.

5:45-6:30pm: You and your friends eat dinner and guess what? The procrastination monster rears its scummy little head and you and your friends decide to get an early start on the night and head over to the pub.

Congratulations Saturday is over for you and out of 14 hours of potential study time (8am -10pm) you have studied for 45 minutes. In addition you did not really enjoy yourself because you were not partying on QLT, Quality Leisure Time. If you think time flies on a Saturday, think about time on a weekday when you have classes to attend. In addition, Saturdays could be a game day and guess what ? College students do not bring their books to the stadium!

So it is extremely important to use the Scheduling tips in Chapter 12 and make use of Quality Leisure Time (QLT) and Quality Study Time (QST). Remember, your tests will come in cycles such as 3 1/2 weeks of reading and lectures then a test. You must stay on top of things so you are not cramming four weeks of four classes and material into four nights.

Hey, What About. . . ?

More Stuff to Worry About

☐ Read it. . . _____

_____

_____

☐ Check It Out. . . _____

_____

_____

☐ Fill It Out. . . _____

_____

_____

☐ Think About It. . . _____

_____

_____

SUMMARY AND MAJOR MAXIMS

Summary & Major Maxims:

All right, you finished the book, now you can either hang on to it for a lifelong reference guide looking at it when you are 85 to see what you were thinking when you were 17 or you can toss it in the box in the basement with other remnants of years gone by such as headless barbie dolls, old hotwheel tracks and little green plastic army men which can still be found to this day in your old sandbox. If you are going to throw it away, make sure you recycle this baby again, you already helped plant some trees by buying this book!

For most of you, never again will you have as much freedom as you will have in college. Be selfish in college, get yourself the best education you can, travel or do the things you always wanted to do, give yourself the healthiest lifestyle possible! Take good care of yourself, actually take great care of yourself and terms of getting the most out of your classes, meeting great friends and working hard to improve yourself!

1. College is the best chance any high school senior has to assure he or she will be given the opportunity to get exactly what he or she want out of life.

2. The most important rule for students embarking on their college selection and application process is to utilize a guidance counselor to the maximum.

3. Remember, while participating in any of life's activities, put the most you can into everything you do!! There are two old sayings which when translated into the 20th century read "Don't torch any bridges and "Treat others like you would want to be treated". Do your best at

everything you do, whether it be washing dishes, stocking groceries or flipping burgers. And always treat other people just like you would want to be treated.

4. All colleges have minimum academic requirements. Check with your academic counselor as early as possible to make sure you are taking the required courses necessary for college admission and are meeting the grade requirements.

5. The best way to take any college exam or quiz is to be ready.

6. There is one secret to writing papers, whether they are mega research papers or one page critiques of a reading assignment, it will make the difference between a fun project and a project from hell. Start them the day they are assigned.

7. Support your friends, be happy for their successes. Compete against the books not your friends or other students.

8. If someone is not giving you the consideration and time you feel you deserve or are willing to give them, find someone who will.

9. The best thing you can do for a high school relationship while in college, is to take great care of yourself.

10. Although you should be outgoing to meet people, it is a good idea when surrounded with new faces to simply listen more than you talk, this way you can sort out the losers, jerks and scums from the cool people.

11. Your key to handling anything that college throws at you, is your attitude.

12. Whenever confronted with something which "bums you out", is a "mental downer" or "depresses you to the max" then simply begin to do just one little productive thing.

13. If you choose to not go immediately on to college, then whatever you do, do not sit around vegging and waste your year off from school. This is the worst thing you could do!!!!!

14. Do not take your books on breaks.

15. Always, always, always, always ask to borrow something and return or repay whatever you borrow in a timely manner!!!!!!!!!!

16. Make absolutely sure you have every single piece of information required on your person before you get into line to register.

17. No matter what, find a physical hobby!

18. Whatever you do, do not miss the review class right before a test!!

19. One great rule of thumb is to complete all reading assignments prior to the lecture.

20. Procrastination is definitely one of your biggest enemies in college and it does lurk around every corner day and night. Putting things off until the last minute will give you a MBA or Major Bad Attitude

21. Do not, under any circumstances, let yourself or your friends drive drunk. Never, not even once.

22. The transition from reading to understanding to knowing takes time.

23. Whatever you do, do not leave your highschool without learning how to use the library.

Add your own:

_____

_____

_____

_____

_____

_____

_____

_____

Whatever happened to the Couch Potato couples?

Whatever happened to the Super Perfect Pairs?

GLOSSARY

ACH (Achievement Tests) are multiple choice exams which test the students' achievement in a specific subject such as English Composition, Biology, Chemistry, Physics, Math: Level I & II, French, Spanish, Italian, German, Latin, Hebrew, American History, European History, Literature

ACT (American College Test) is a four part test consisting of the following sections: English, Mathematics Test, Reading Test and Science Reasoning Test . The test is taken primarily for admissions.

Ample cash horde: Having enough money to finance your college education or at least buy a pizza whenever you want.

Boreboxes: Endearing term referring to a classroom.

Brain Drain: The reduction of mental concentration power caused by prolonged and reoccurring intense lecture sessions.

Cab Tab Fund: A fund set up on a dorm floor, in a fraternity, sorority or among any group of friends to provide money for cab fairs for students who have been responsible enough to strand themselves and should not be driving. Everyone pitches in and the users of the service reimburse the fund every time they use it.

CLEP: This the College Level Examination Program. This program will give college credits based on scores received on 2 kinds of test. (1) Five general exams covering English composition, math, natural sciences, social sciences and humanities and (2) subject exams covering 41 areas.

College-Work Study Program (CWS): A government-supported program which provides part-time jobs to students who need help paying college expenses. Work-study jobs are awarded to the students by the financial aid office.

CRP (Casual Review Period): A period of time which is set aside to casually review a course's material. This could be a week or two before an exam or at any time during the semester. By marking down a review schedule on your calendar and reviewing previously covered chapters on a casual non rush basis you allow yourself plenty of time to master all the material which allows you to take any test completely relaxed and confident in your ability to do well.

Deadline: A date given for certain registrations and submission of college application and testing material. You should subtract five weeks from the date provided to get your true deadline date, making sure you get all of your information in early. This is especially true for financial aid applications!

Deferred Admissions: High school seniors may apply and be accepted to a college and then take the year off to work etc.. and attend college the following year.

Early Decision: The process by which a high school senior applies to his or her first choice college by November 1st. You are notified of acceptance by mid-December. If accepted, under early decision, you are required to accept no other institution, and if not, you are deferred to regular decision.

Family Financial Statement (FFS): Need analysis form processed by The American College Testing Program (ACT).

Financial Aid Form (FAF): Need analysis form processed by the College Scholarship Services (CSS).

Grants: Awards based on financial need which do not require repayment. Grants are available through the federal government, state agencies, and educational institutions.

LBC or Library Base Camp: A study station usually set up in the library . It consist of students opening their books into the Optima Study Position in what appears to be preparation for studying only to leave them to collect dust as they scope out who else is in the library.

MBA: Major Bad Attitude or Master of Business Administration.

NPK or No Pressure Knowledge: The kind of knowledge one possesses over something they can do extremely well without really thinking about it. These are things you just do because you know how to and, it is almost second nature, with no pressure. You should prepare for tests until you reach the same No Pressure Knowledge about the material.

Open Admissions: Colleges which admit almost any high school graduates. Most have programs to help students with academic problems.

Optima Study Place: A low traffic, low distraction location and layout for studying. This could be a particular table or study booth in the library. It might be an empty classroom or in your own room with your neatly arranged desk whereby you can study for long durations without distraction.

Optima Study Position: An efficient configuration of student and educational material. This studying layout is a perfect composition of book placement, notebook angling, beverage/munchy supply and access, calculator positioning and writing utensil selection, all orchestrated for the sole purpose of efficient study material placement and can only be ineffective if you forget the most important design factor. This is to put your head down in your book and study.

P-ACT+: is a four part exam testing the following areas: Writing Skills, Mathematics Test, Reading Test, Science Reasoning Test. The test is designed to measure a student's skill and knowledge already acquired in the early years of high school. The P-ACT+ is a great way for students to see where they are at and to help prepare them for the ACT. Highly recommeded!

Paper Buster: A three ring binder designated for organizing and writing papers. This allows the student to collect research material and order it in any fashion they want. (Call 800-222-6462 for three ring binders made out of recycled paperboard)

Pell Grant: Financial assistance, awarded by the federal government on the basis of need. The grant may be used toward tuition, room and board, books, or other educational costs. Requires no repayment.

Perkins Loan: Loans funded by the federal government at a low rate of interest and awarded by the institution. Repayment and interest begin nine months after a student graduates, leaves school, or drops below half-time enrollment.

PITS: Polluting ignorant treemurdering scumbags. Endearing term used when referring to persons or organizations that are not environmentally responsible and do not practice recycling.

PLUS Loan: A loan program (not need based) in which parents can borrow from a bank or other lender. Repayment of principal and interests begins within sixty days of loan disbursement.

PSAT/NMSQT (Preliminary Scholastic Aptitude Test/National Merit Scholarship Qualifying Test): is a multiple choice test that measures verbal and mathematical reasoning abilities important for academic success in college. The sections covered are outlined below under SAT. It is very important to note that the PSAT is used as the basis for selection for the National Merit Scholarship when you are a senior.

QUALITY LEISURE TIME (QLT): Is being able to kick back and do whatever you want, with out having to worry about what you aren't doing or should be doing (homework etc). Otherwise kicking back doing what you want to, without having to worry about what you are putting off to take this time.

QUALITY STUDY TIME (QST): is being able to study utilizing the maximum amount of focused concentration because you have partied or enjoyed your QLT and are anxious to learn and accomplish something academically productive, which like relaxing, is also a natural human desire. With QST you can achieve much greater learning in much less time.

SAT: (The Scholastic Aptitude Test) is a three hour aptitude test. SAT tests ones verbal and mathematical reasoning abilities. It consists of the two sections.

Saturation Lectures: A parental figure communication warfare theory based on utilizing a continual and repetitive series of speeches and verbal exchanges designed to instill information and impart advice to its target audience by wearing their ears down to such a degree that the target audience has no choice but to listen and say yes at 30 second intervals.

This tactic is usually employed by parental figures while trapping their target audience in bathroom doorways, before going out for an evening or during long distance college phone calls.

Self-inflicted stranding: An incredibly intelligent human survival technique whereby responsible persons who are irresponsibly intoxicated strand themselves and make it impossible for them to drive.

Skipping frenzies: A dangerous pattern of missing classes which starts by missing just one class and then leads to another and then another, until a student misses more classes then he attends.

Speed drilling: A rapid fire lecture technique employed by some college professors in which they cram an enormous amount of material and notes into one class fully expecting the students to hear, write down and understand every word.

Stafford Loan: A loan program in which eligible students may borrow from a bank or other financial institution. The federal government pays the interest on the loan while the student is in school. Repayment and interest begin six months after the student graduates, leaves school, or drops below half-time enrollment.

Supplemental Educational Opportunity Grant Program (SEOG): SEOGS are provided to a limited number of undergraduate students with financial need. Preference is given to students with exceptional financial need.

Supplemental Loan for Students (SLS): A loan program (not need based) in which graduate students and self-supporting undergraduate students can borrow from a bank or other lender. Repayment of principal and interest begins within sixty days of loan disbursement.

Syllabus: (short intellectual sounding word meaning: all the stuff you gotta know.)

TVT=Total Vegetation Time: Time when a student participates in some form of low mental and physical impact activity designed to relax..

Voyeuristic Collegiate Vampires (VCV's): Students who prefers to study at night.

(Some terms excerpted from The College Board's ACT handouts on Financial Aid)

One final note about going to college, people and this planet. It's a simple rule: If there is no oxygen, you're dead!!! So no matter where you live, in a dorm, fraternity or sorority house, off campus or at home, start a recycling program. Talk to your resident director and resident assistants and establish a recycling program in your dorm. Set one up for your fraternity or sorority. Go to the college president and start one for the whole campus, dorms, classroom buildings, cafeteria, Greek system, the whole place. This would be a great resume building project and you would be doing the environment a world of good. When you are talking to your parents about college, this book, or just life in general, talk to them about starting to recycle at your home. In fact, refuse to buy things from or deal with anyone or any business that does not actively recycle. Set up monitoring procedures in your dorm, house, campus or job and punish those polluting ignorant treemurdering scumbags "PITS" who do not adhere to environmentally responsible disposal practices.

If you want to improve your reading skills and your quality of life then check out:

"50 Simple Things You Can Do To Save The Earth"

or

"The Student Environmental Action Guide", by the Student Environmental Coalition. An environmental handbook written for students by students.

All available from The Earthworks Group, 1400 Shattuck Ave. #25, Berkeley, CA 94709 (510) 652-8533.

Later on!

ADDRESS BOOK

Don't forget to bring with you to college your most valuable high school asset: your friends!

- Name_____
- Address_____

_____
- City_____State_____
- Zip_____Birthdate_____

Phone number
H:
W:

- Name_____
- Address_____

_____
- City_____State_____
- Zip_____Birthdate_____

Phone number
H:
W:

- Name_____
- Address_____

_____
- City_____State_____
- Zip_____Birthdate_____

Phone number
H:
W:

- Name_____
- Address_____

_____
- City_____State_____
- Zip_____Birthdate_____

Phone number
H:
W:

- Name_____
- Address_____

Phone number
H:
W:

- City_____State_____
- Zip_____Birthdate_____

- Name_____
- Address_____

Phone number
H:
W:

- City_____State_____
- Zip_____Birthdate_____

- Name_____
- Address_____

Phone number
H:
W:

- City_____State_____
- Zip_____Birthdate_____

- Name_____
- Address_____

Phone number
H:
W:

- City_____State_____
- Zip_____Birthdate_____

- Name_____
- Address_____

Phone number
H:
W:

- City_____State_____
- Zip_____Birthdate_____

- Name_____
- Address_____

Phone number
H:
W:

- City_____State_____
- Zip_____Birthdate_____

- Name_____
- Address_____

Phone number
H:
W:

- City_____State_____
- Zip_____Birthdate_____

- Name_____
- Address_____

Phone number
H:
W:

- City_____State_____
- Zip_____Birthdate_____

- Name_____
- Address_____
  _____
- City_____ State_____
- Zip_____ Birthdate_____

| **Phone number** |
| H: |
| W: |

- Name_____
- Address_____
  _____
- City_____ State_____
- Zip_____ Birthdate_____

| **Phone number** |
| H: |
| W: |

- Name_____
- Address_____
  _____
- City_____ State_____
- Zip_____ Birthdate_____

| **Phone number** |
| H: |
| W: |

- Name_____
- Address_____
  _____
- City_____ State_____
- Zip_____ Birthdate_____

| **Phone number** |
| H: |
| W: |

- Name_____
- Address_____
  _____
- City_____ State_____
- Zip_____ Birthdate_____

| **Phone number** |
| H: |
| W: |

- Name_____
- Address_____
  _____
- City_____ State_____
- Zip_____ Birthdate_____

| **Phone number** |
| H: |
| W: |

- Name_____
- Address_____
  _____
- City_____ State_____
- Zip_____ Birthdate_____

| **Phone number** |
| H: |
| W: |

- Name_____
- Address_____
  _____
- City_____ State_____
- Zip_____ Birthdate_____

| **Phone number** |
| H: |
| W: |

Address Book

- Name_____

- Address_____

  _____

- City_____State_____

- Zip_____Birthdate_____

Phone number

H:

W:

- Name_____

- Address_____

  _____

- City_____State_____

- Zip_____Birthdate_____

Phone number

H:

W:

- Name_____

- Address_____

  _____

- City_____State_____

- Zip_____Birthdate_____

Phone number

H:

W:

- Name_____

- Address_____

  _____

- City_____State_____

- Zip_____Birthdate_____

Phone number

H:

W:

- Name_____

- Address_____

  _____

- City_____State_____

- Zip_____Birthdate_____

Phone number

H:

W:

- Name_____

- Address_____

  _____

- City_____State_____

- Zip_____Birthdate_____

Phone number

H:

W:

- Name_____

- Address_____

  _____

- City_____State_____

- Zip_____Birthdate_____

Phone number

H:

W:

- Name_____

- Address_____

  _____

- City_____State_____

- Zip_____Birthdate_____

Phone number

H:

W: